Look Up – Way Up!

THE FRIENDLY GIANT

The Biography of Robert M. Homme

Grant D. Fairley

Published By: Palantir Publishing - a division of McK Consulting Inc.
Toronto ~ Windsor ~ Chicago

ISBN 978-0-9780275-0-6

Cover design by Cari Fairley of Artist's Tree, www.artiststree.ca
Publication production assistance by SOHO Creative, www.sohocreative.com

Printed in the United States of America

Contents

Dedication

This book is dedicated to my mother Lois Ann Fairley who passed away this summer after a short battle with cancer. We all miss you mom. She like so many parents introduced me to imagination, faith, hope and love – and The Friendly Giant.

Acknowledgments

I would like to thank Bob and Esther Homme for their cooperation and enthusiasm for this project. My wife Cari and I have enjoyed their hospitality and getting to know them. It is our privilege to introduce the readers to these people and the story of The Friendly Giant in a deeper way.

Many people have contributed their memories, ideas and perspectives. Rod Coneybeare, Holly Larocque, the late Ernie Coombs and the late Dr. Fred Rainsberry have made significant contributions. Many others have shared their thoughts and memories that are appreciated.

Gary Carter and his team at Kainos Enterprises have been invaluable with their insight and editing assistance.

It has been a good investment to have a daughter in the history program at the University of Western Ontario. Beth has been a great help in pushing this project over the finish line with her assistance in editing and overall comments on flow and content.

Palantir Publishing took this project completed in 1999 to finally a book to share in 2007.

My talented and beautiful wife gets the appropriate credit for the cover design and artwork. She also was the one who believed that this needed to be published and never gave up hope in spite of the disappointments and challenges along the way.

Special thanks go to my parents who like so many parents in Canada and the United States had the foresight to introduce us to The Friendly Giant when we were preschoolers. Great choice!

Transgenerationally, I would thank my children, Doug, Beth, Emma & Scott who gave us a new reason to watch Friendly again and to see anew the impact on them we felt a generation ago.

Preface

I magine spending time with someone who was a special part of your childhood. Unlike so many of life's adult experiences, meeting The Friendly Giant a.k.a. Bob Homme did not disappoint. Bob was Friendly and Friendly was Bob in so many ways. All of the qualities that endeared The Friendly Giant to generations of children and the adults who watched along are a part of this person. This book was a real joy to create.

The book is not intended as a textbook treatment of Bob Homme and his gift to us – The Friendly Giant. Some of that is covered in the book on the history of children's television by Dr. Fred Rainsberry, A History of Children's Television In English Canada 1952-1986, mentioned later. This journey is through the eyes of the child in all of us still sitting in front of our old television watching Friendly. The challenge of this book for the reader will be to float back in time to that childhood, "Not far away – not long ago." Regardless of how idyllic – or painful – those years may have been for you, Friendly represents a positive experience connecting three generations of children growing up in Canada and the United States. I hope that you will learn some of the little known trivia behind the show. More important is the story of this great man who reached through the glass of the television sets of our childhood and brought us into his castle to sit at his fireplace.

As the years have gone by (without any of us getting any older of course), I have had the pleasure of introducing our friends the Giant, Rusty and

Jerome to my children Doug, Beth, Emma & Scott. Watching them wander into the castle and choose a chair by that fireplace links our childhoods in time even though the times of our generations are so different.

In speaking with my parents about it, they remember the same feeling seeing the three Fairley boys grow up with The Friendly Giant all those years ago. Mom knew it was a good place for us to be when we were with Rusty, Jerome and Friendly. Both parents made time to watch Friendly with us so that the show was something we shared together.

While there is no Mrs. Friendly Giant in the castle on television, I am pleased to report that Bob was married to someone as delightful as The Friendly Giant would have married. Esther Homme is integral to the story of Bob's life and his show.

Sadly, Bob Homme died in May 2000 at the age of 81 but not before he received The Order of Canada in 1998 – Canada's highest civilian honour for his lifetime contribution to Canada. He is such a part of the English language Canadian psyche because we met him in our preschool years and he was there for us whenever we were home sick or for summer vacations on CBC. As I'll discuss later, to truly understand what it means to grow up as an English Canadian from 1958 to the mid-1990s, you must include The Friendly Giant in the tale. The award is a fitting recognition of that fact.

The same is also true for children in the United States who grew up with Friendly from 1954 until 1968 on National Educational Television (NET) which is now known as the Public Broadcasting Service (PBS) after 1970. NET was only two years old when Friendly began, making it one of their earliest children's programs.

Today, if you want to rekindle those feelings and thoughts about The Friendly Giant, you can visit the CBC Museum at the CBC headquarters in Toronto. It houses the familiar Friendly Giant memorabilia. When on display, you can see the Friendly Giant costume, recorder, Rusty and Jerome, the fireplace and tiny furniture along with some of the other pieces of the show. It is a great place to visit. They also have a sample show available to watch as part of a tribute to the CBC's golden era of children's television.

You may also enjoy some audio clips from my interviews done with Bob at his home after his retirement in preparation of this book. A few years later and I would have had these interviews on a digital camera. But at the time the old audio cassettes were the tool of choice. As I have learned from re-watching the shows and from Bob himself, it was the strength of the audio presentation of The Friendly Giant that enchanted in spite of the great visual memories that we have as well of the show. You may listen to these audio clips at www.palantir-publishing.com. I would also invite you to send along your thoughts and memories of Friendly as a child, parent or grandparent. As this book is created digitally, future updates can include additional material and contributions from the extended family of those who loved The Friendly Giant.

I regret that at present, there are no rebroadcasts of The Friendly Giant to watch with another generation of children. The shows are also not available on video or DVD. Hopefully they will be some day. Having recently reviewed some of the old videos I taped on VHS, the shows do what all great literature, music and entertainment do; they stand the test of time.

While Bob is gone, the gift he gave us of the Friendly Giant lives on in not just the museums and video but in the lives of all the children, their parents and grandparents who shared their mornings "Looking up – way up!"

Giant Fans

"Like millions of other Canadians I have fond memories of growing up watching The Friendly Giant. And still today, I find the words 'Look up – Way Up' as part of my vocabulary.

I guess my most lasting memory will always be the fact that in the early to mid 80s I had the opportunity of actually sharing a studio with Friendly. I'd spend my evenings reading The National in Studio 2 at the old Jarvis Street building in Toronto, the same studio Bob would use to tape his program.

And I must say it was somehow relaxing at night looking into the camera dealing with the weighty issues of the world's news yet also seeing out of the corner of my eye, Rusty, and the castle wall. It was very comforting!"

Peter Mansbridge, Chief Correspondent, CBC TV News

1

Look Back – Way Back

Mention the phrase, "Look up... way up!" and you'll either be greeted with a questioning look or a warm glow of childhood memory "and I'll call Rusty". Those who watched Bob Homme as The Friendly Giant on television have that very deep response that opens doors from many years ago when they and their world was young.

For those who did not have The Friendly Giant as part of their preschool days in Canada or the United States, it is difficult to explain how important he was for us who knew about Friendly, Rusty and Jerome. It's a bit like explaining the feeling you have when you hear "Hockey Night In Canada" music playing. If you're old enough, you can imagine George Armstrong, Johnny Bower, Dave Keon and the Toronto Maple Leafs winning the Stanley Cup. If you're too young to remember 1967, you can't quite make the same connection about the glory days of the Original Six and the Leafs winning. But I digress....

For those who knew Friendly when they were young children, come with me on a trip back to your preschool days or those of your children. Walk through the mist of memory and be transported into those memories right now. Remember the sights and sounds of sitting in front of your old television set with tubes glowing in the back. Perhaps you had a black and white television. Was it a playroom in your basement? The living room? What do you remember about that room? Can you recall the furniture that was a part of those early days of your life? Are there any smells from your childhood that connect you to those moments?

If you are a parent or grandparent, perhaps your memories are of seeing your child or children sitting on the old sofa in front of the television. Does it seem possible that they have grown up? How the years fly by. Those little wide-eyed wonders are now finishing university, out in the working world or may have preschoolers of their own!

For many of us The Friendly Giant reminds us of a time when our moms could stay home and our little world was secure. For others, it was a safe and quiet place to be in a troubled home. In Friendly, they saw a thoughtful and caring parent and later grandparent figure who spoke gently and was interested in them. Friendly, Rusty and Jerome took time to chat with you, read you books, introduce you to music and convey the comfort of a good place to be. The outgoing Jerome and the more introverted Rusty were performed with such ease by the master of voices and ad lib, Rod Coneybeare. The dynamic was one of fun. It is a place you wanted to be. Each of these characters had a wonderful laugh that was infectious to hear and connected with the audience whether young or old.

While so much of the television world of every generation was fun to watch, it was usually an external experience. We were watching them; we were not with them. One of the magical differences intentionally created by Bob Homme in The Friendly Giant program was the sense of intimacy that you felt. You were not just watching the television; you were with him. You had crossed the drawbridge, gone through the big doors and were now in the castle too.

So let's return to that fairer time when our weekday mornings were not rushed and we did not reach for a cup of coffee. Instead we were ready to visit a castle with a friendly giant, a rooster, a giraffe, some music and great books. A warm memory awaits!

2

Cocoa & Cinnamon Toast

What do you get when you mix music, stories, a rooster, a boot, farms, a castle, a giraffe and a giant? It is a recipe for wonder, delight and fun for all ages. For many children, parents and grandparents in the United States and Canada it was a daily visit with The Friendly Giant. For fifteen minutes each weekday morning, everyone was welcome to read a book or enjoy a concert in the giant's castle.

The nostalgia of those visits continues for the generations who spent their preschool mornings with Jerome the giraffe, Rusty the rooster and The Friendly Giant. See a clip online or hear a reference to Friendly on a CBC or PBS history moment and suddenly you are a preschooler again.

So many cues bring back the warm feelings. The sounds of that musical instrument, the recorder, playing Early One Morning touch somewhere deep in the memory of children and their parents and grandparents who watched the show together. The sight of the castle drawbridge lowering revealing the two great front doors that said Friendly Giant or the very important early decision of which chair to choose are all strong emotional touchstones for us.

Say the words, "Look Up – Way Up!" in public and expect to hear the response, "…and I'll call Rusty." These images and experiences are strongly ingrained in the psyche of the baby-boomers and members of busters and even some of the boomer-echo and Gen-X who saw Friendly in reruns.

Bob Homme as The Friendly Giant had a unique ability to create a sense of intimacy and relationship with his viewers. That is perhaps why we still have this powerful bond with Friendly on such a deep level. Like tastes and smells of our childhood, there is something different about these early impressions. It is something like the experience of smelling bread or cookies baking at home. For some it is visiting a childhood camp or cottage years later where the sights and smells take us back to our distant past. Something stirs the child within us.

For children who were born in the 1950s or later, it is refreshing to be four or five years old again. Life certainly seemed less complicated then. Bob Homme's story is a remarkable one. His story is that of a very special man who was truly as delightful in person as you remember him on television. That is one of the secrets of why The Friendly Giant has such a special place in the hearts of all the children who grew up with him.

Friendly was Bob and Bob was Friendly.

Bob Homme always respected his audience – especially the preschoolers and primary grade viewers. He hoped that our quarter hour at the castle would be a time of listening, wondering and fun. It would not be the over-the-top slapstick antics of a Howdy Doody. It would be a slower pace than Captain Kangaroo. Like the man himself, the character of Friendly would be unique and personal. It reflected the kind of values and commitment that Bob had to the quality of the experience for his young audience.

So it was fitting that one of the first things he did was to give each member of the audience the opportunity to choose. Do you remember which chair you chose each morning? Was it a chair for one of you or a big armchair for two of you to curl up in or a rocking chair for one who likes to rock in the middle? Grab a cup of cocoa and some cinnamon toast. Let the preschoolers in you wander back to our simpler times around a black and white television set with rabbit ears. Welcome back to the wonderful world of The Friendly Giant.

"These are important memories that I wish the next generation also held."

Fred Penner Children's Entertainer and beloved troubadour from
CBC's Fred Penner's Place

3

Once Upon A Time ...

From the distance came a familiar reassuring voice. We could not see him but we knew he was there.

"Once upon a time, not long ago, not far away ..."

With those words, children and adults knew that they were now in the land of The Friendly Giant. It was the giant who was speaking. The camera panned across a scene.

Some days it was a farm complete with animals and dirt roads set on some rolling hills. The cows were grazing. A barnyard might have some pigs or chickens making their sounds. A farm tractor or truck might be on the move.

In one episode there was an explosion as blasting cleared rocks in road construction. For a night theme the show began with the moon already up over the castle. Other shows opened at the airport with the planes ready for takeoff. The aircraft came in different sizes. A very busy control tower could be seen.

Occasionally, a night scene greeted the viewers as a segue into a bed-time story or a concert about the night sky and stars.

One of my favourites was the small town with the shops and homes. For an instant we felt like giants as we too looked down and noticed the people and places on the set. Perhaps if we looked a little harder we could even see in the shop windows.

A viewer favorite was the railway set or the harbor scene. The craftsmanship and sound effects of the setting added to the delight. Occasionally the scene might be more exotic like a jungle or a desert. All were designed to bring a point of reference to the child's experience.

All this was viewed with the rich tones of the unseen Friendly describing what was there. We learned to pay attention to those opening moments. Usually our visit in the castle would explore a topic suggested in that first scene. Perhaps it was watching the horses, listening to the sound of a chain-saw or watching a tugboat in the harbour.

Then you saw it. You knew that it would be there. It was always there. But there was always a moment of excitement every time it came into view.

There's that boot.

Big boot.

It made everything around him look very small.

Then came the invitation every child – and the child in every adult – loved to hear.

"Look up – way up!"

There was that familiar friend. The white hair and the warm smile. Giant boots and giant clothes of yellow and brown. His bright eyes sparkled and never without a warm smile. Yes. Definitely a friendly giant.

"We're on our way to the castle."

"I'll go first and let the drawbridge down and open the big front doors for you."

"Are you ready?"

"Here's my castle."

"I loved The Friendly Giant! I used to want to be so close to him that I sat right in front of the TV. My parents used to pick me up and move me back.

It is said that friends you make in your childhood have a very special place throughout your life. They were friends when you were just a kid often before any triumphs and tragedies shaped who we are. For many, we lose touch with those people of long ago where we shared the adventure of our brave new world.

I wanted to be tall like Friendly."

Ann Rohmer, Host, Breakfast Television, City TV

4

Early One Morning – Many Mornings

Then to the sound of the old tune, Early One Morning, we now see the castle. The castle flags might be blue or red or white. Some mornings the castle had snow on the turrets – other days not. The camera closes in on the lowering drawbridge. The two front doors show the name FRIENDLY GIANT. Slowly they open.

Yes. We are definitely at the right place.

"Here we are inside."

Now we gather at the familiar and cozy room with the fireplace. The giant's great hand is there dwarfing the room. Friendly sets the chairs up for us.

"Here's one little chair for one of you ..."

"...and a bigger chair for two more to curl up in."

"...and a rocking chair for someone who likes to rock."

You then scrambled in your minds to get into your favourite chair. I preferred the "big arm chair for two to curl up in." The chairs face the fireplace with the sketch of the castle over the mantle. Two dogs sit on either side of the clock. Bracketing them is the candelabras. The hutch is on the left and the bookshelf waits on the right. There are many books at this castle. A little table by the chairs is just the right size for a cup of cocoa and some cinnamon toast.

"Look up – way up – and I'll call Rusty."

"Rusty!"

Now as we are looking at a castle wall with a window, a rooster appears out of a cloth bag hanging on the wall. This is Rusty wearing his traditional polka-dot shirt. The sack we learn is "The Book Bag" where Rusty lives. It is Rusty's turn to speak with that very high and enthusiastic voice.

"Hello Friendly."

"Where have you been and what have you seen?"

A conversation follows about the topic of the day. Often Friendly reports to his favourite rooster what is happening in the world outside the castle. Then the conversation turns to their missing friend.

"Where's Jerome?"

Instantly we hear the whistle that we all tried to master when we were growing up. Through the large window of the castle appears the head of Jerome the giraffe – always ready for action and a good time.

What follows might be a book on the topic of the day. If it was a music day, the episodes often meant a trip to the next room for a concert. There the musical raccoons, Patty and Polly are waiting. Angie and Fiddle are the talented cats who might also join in on the concert with Rusty, Jerome and Friendly.

5

Grown-up Kids – Sort of ...

For fourteen years in the United States on National Educational Television the forerunner to the Public Broadcasting System (PBS) and for twenty-eight years in Canada on the Canadian Broadcasting Corporation (CBC), children could visit their favourite castle and their favourite giant.

More than forty years after it began, The Friendly Giant continued in syndication in Canada and the United States.

I was one of the many children who visited the castle of a giant. Our mornings as preschoolers included this adventure every weekday. One did not have to be especially brave to visit this giant because he was a friendly giant.

For children there were many big and scary things in our world of the late fifties and early sixties. Along with the usual challenges of very tall adults in crowds and cars driving down our road, we were living through the deep freeze of the cold war. We were doing the "duck and cover" drills in our schools to prepare for a nuclear attack. It seems funny now – knowing how that would not have helped if there really was a nuclear attack but back then it was serious business.

There were wonderful encounters on television too. Children saw rocket launches with astronauts. Cowboys could appear at any time.

Depending on your age, you may have grown up with Sherri Lewis & Lambchop, Kukla, Fran & Ollie, Chez Helene, Mr. Dressup, Soupy Sales, Butternut Square, Captain Kangaroo, Razzle Dazzle, Bozo The Clown, Howdy Doody, The Mickey Mouse Club, Lassie and Romper Room. The cartoons might have included Bugs Bunny, Popeye, The Jetsons, The Mighty Hercules, Quick Draw McGraw, Beanie & Cecil Huckleberry Hound, Mighty Mouse, Felix the Cat and Kimba the White Lion. Various claymation or puppet shows like Davey & Goliath, Gumby or The New Adventures of Pinocchio were part of our early mornings or afternoons.

Later arrivals might have watched Seasame Street, Mr. Roger's Neighborhood, Under The Umbrella Tree, The Muppet Show, Fred Penner, The Elephant Show and Size Small. Mr. Dressup was still on too. Their cartoons could have been the Care Bears, Tale Spin, Teddy Ruxpin, Chip & Dale Rescue Rangers and still Bugs Bunny. Claymation types of shows included Postman Pat, Charlie Chalk and Thomas the Tank Engine.

To a child, television was an amazing contraption with all those glowing tubes in the back of the set. Setting the antennas became my specialty; those rabbit ears had to be just right. These are now just a memory in the age of digital cable and satellite signals – unless you have an old television at your cottage. Then those early skills (and usually tin foil) are particularly useful.

So many images and experiences of our generation came through this newly established medium of information, culture and worldview. It would take many years to begin to understand the potency of this thing called a TV.

Watching The Friendly Giant was an important balance to some of the other pressures of that time. Friendly's castle was a safe and warm place to be. Although the giant was really tall he always had a warm smile and a gentle hand outstretched toward us. It was quite a thing for little people like us to be friends with a real giant.

One of the few disappointments of growing older in school was that you were not home when Friendly was on. This of course was years before VHS tapes or DVDs to record the shows you missed. If you were not watching, you missed it! No second chances with technology of the 60s. That meant that we couldn't visit the castle since that magic window to Friendly occurred when school was on. But we were able to visit with The Friendly Giant whenever we were home sick from school or on holidays. Even though we didn't see him as often, we knew that he was always there.

"My kids remember Friendly when I was playing in Sudbury. We had driven up from Springfield, MA to play for the Wolves of the E.P.H.L. Friendly, Rusty & Jerome were a hit, not only for Canadian kids but my American kids too. It makes you wonder why they would not keep going with such a great show. I guess there's not enough bodies and blood flying around. Our family loved the music, the set, but mostly the lovely way Bob talked to the kids. I wish he was back.

People say I look like Friendly. This is a true story. I was standing in line at an airport waiting for a ticket. This old couple was in front and the old lady kept looking back at me. So the old fellow asked his wife, 'You know this guy?' She said, 'Yes, I see him on TV all the time.' So I'm getting ready to sign the usual autograph and the old guy says, 'Who is he?' The old lady says, 'He's The Friendly Giant.' Did I also say that Friendly was good looking too?"

Don Cherry, Hockey Coach & Commentator

6

Past and Present Together

My wife Cari and I journeyed down the country road near Grafton, Ontario. It was Cari's first visit with Bob and Esther Homme in their home. Anticipation. Once again there would be that warm, safe, cozy feeling from watching the show. A childhood dream was coming true. What would it be like? Cari, a normally poised person ready to meet anyone, was nervous. It was exciting for her to think of finally meeting this very special person from her childhood.

It was a strange convergence of past and present for anyone who had the opportunity to meet Bob. Would it be like Star Trek's dire warnings that the past and present must never meet or catastrophe would strike? What would he really sound like? How much different would he be from the Friendly of her childhood?

There was tingling curiosity. We turned up their laneway and there was the house surrounded by trees. There were many flowers demonstrating Esther's enthusiasm for gardening. This lovely summer day suited a visit with Friendly.

Getting out of the car, we were met by Molly, their cute Springer spaniel. Not far behind were Esther and Bob. Wide-eyed, Cari met this person of her past who was now part of her present too. While the glasses Bob was then wearing were not familiar, the rich tones of his voice instantly transported Cari back to her preschool days.

Esther was a perfect match for his gracious and caring personality. Following the introductions we enjoyed lunch at their long table. Looking to the deck, we could see the many birds feeding outside the window. The birds were always welcome. Bob and Esther were delightful people to be with. It was truly enchanting.

After lunch, we went down to the basement office area complete with a wood stove. It was strange to see Friendly using a computer – obviously a thoroughly modern giant. Then we looked at some of the icons of our past. Out of the box came Rusty (and his stunt double!) and the giraffe with all his gusto, Jerome. It was a strange feeling to hold Rusty and Jerome on our hands. We really expected them to start talking. Where was Rod Coneybeare when you needed him?

There were the small chairs gathered around the fireplace. The tiny hutch sat on the one side and the small book case was on the other side of the fire. The painting of the castle hung overhead. The two miniature candelabras with the small dogs and the clock all graced the tiny mantle. We marveled at how small they really are. Was it the child in us still imagining the giant context in the castle? Perhaps it was feeling that we had sat in those chairs so many times. Fantasy met reality and survived the meeting.

The giant's "pipes" hung on the wall. They were a wonderful collection of beautiful wooden recorders. Bob sat down and pulled out his clarinet. Sitting back, we listened to the master make the clarinet come alive as he shared so many melodies.

The room contained numerous awards received for his innovation and commitment to excellence in the area of children's television and education. The show received the prestigious Ohio State Award for broadcasting four years in a row.

We looked at a scrap book filled with pictures and clippings about The Friendly Giant. There were some outlines for shows done many years before.

Especially valued by Bob was mail from those who watched Friendly. Some were written by parents on behalf of their preschool children. Others were the work of the kids themselves.

Next it was off to the upper room over the garage that housed the icons for so many of our memories. There on one side of the room was the castle. Bob asked us to wait until he was in position. Then as transformed into Friendly once more, he did his classic opening lines to the show as he lowered the drawbridge and opened the big front doors. We both stood there mesmerized like the five year olds we once were.

The room also housed props and all the books ever used on the shows. Listening to Bob describe how he developed the focus of each program reminded Cari of the same process used in any excellent preschool teaching model.

Off we went in his four wheel drive vehicle. We toured the beautiful acreage where they lived. There were a couple of ponds and a beautiful view of the surrounding countryside with the farms and forests. It looked very much like an opening scene for The Friendly Giant.

Part of the joy of the visit came from the many stories and anecdotes Bob and Esther shared. It was something magical to hear. But even as I describe these moments from a summer day, it is such a two-dimensional expression of what was a richly textured experience. Similar to the difference between a picture and being there, I can only try to tell you what it was truly like. But for those who loved the program, imagine how nice it would be to spend time with Friendly. It is all of that and more.

"It was a good show for preschoolers. Good relationships were modeled. Each was interested in what the others had to say. There was a strong sense of dependability. Good music and stories in the program. We occasionally played practical jokes between our show in Studio 1 and Bob's in Studio 2. Bob created a quiet and trusting relationship with his audience. The gentle ending of each show was reassuring."

Ernie Coombs, Mr. Dressup, CBC television

7

Giant Thinking

How did ~~what was to become~~ The Friendly Giant begin?

Bob Homme (pronounced "hummy") graduated from the University of Wisconsin with a major in Economics. But instead of some of the typical plans for an economics major, Bob was headed in a different direction. Following graduation, Bob pursued his passion. He took a job with the University of Wisconsin State Radio Station WHA. Radio had long been Bob's first love.

Bob grew up in the golden age of radio where the imagination could thrive with the voices, music and sound effects of the story tellers of the day. Radio was an interactive medium requiring the listener to fill in so many of the details and pictures using the imagination. Those who were gifted in radio productions knew how to stimulate their audiences to imagine, think and dream.

Knowing that the future was going to be in television more than his beloved radio, Bob wanted to learn more than he could in his limited role at the community station. Better training came from observing the big productions.

At that point, he was working part-time at the university radio station, and a booth announcer on the community television station. From his experiences in radio, he believed that he could create a program of music for commercial use. As he explored this concept, he was put in touch with MUZAK a concept and a company then in its infancy. Bob arranged to represent MUZAK in the Milwaukee, Wisconsin area. Bob was going from dentist's office to doctor's office with this musical product. The usual result was that Bob would be in a "blue funk." It was not long before he realized that selling was not a place where he would either make money or have much fun. But with a growing family, he worked away at it.

Watching from the balcony of the huge Chicago Merchandise Mart became an important and enjoyable past-time for Bob and some of his friends. On Sunday mornings driving two hours from Madison in Chicago, people could see the rehearsals of the very popular "The Dave Garroway Show." This television variety show included many big names in the entertainment world. Peering down on the set, Bob and friends could watch what went into "Network Television" at that time. There were few technical tricks but there was a lot of imagination. It was also a great place to be entertained and inspired.

The trip back included a stop at a restaurant with a television to see the finished product from Chicago they had just seen rehearsed. It was stimulating to this young man who had a passion to use his creativity. Bob had developed an interest in programming.

Then it was while driving back from Chicago to Madison, Wisconsin in 1953 that a life-changing insight struck Bob. It is amazing to think how important a typical drive home can be. For Bob, a sudden insight that struck him in that discouragement was a real inspiration, "If the set and props are miniatures, then I can be a giant!"

That was an idea that would work on television. If they are miniatures, then I am a giant. At that time there were no giants on television. The Jolly Green Giant of the vegetable variety had not yet moved from radio to television.

Like so many great ideas, Bob didn't know where this one came from but there it was in his mind. That was it. He would be a giant. However, he would be a kind giant, not a nasty one.

One of the problems with a really great idea is that someone else might agree with you. They might take your excellent idea and make it happen before you can do so yourself. Who better to talk to than a spouse? Bob arrived home and it was clear to his wife Esther that something was up.

Bob explained the idea of a children's show featuring himself as a giant surrounded by miniatures. She immediately thought it was a great idea. But still he wondered. Would a giant be too scary for children? Esther's answer was, "Not if it is a friendly giant." There it was – The Friendly Giant.

This led to an easy decision. Realizing that the dentists he visited as a MUZAK salesperson would likely sell him an unnecessary set of dentures before he sold them his product, Bob quit.

He approached the program director of the station at the University of Wisconsin and told him about his big idea. His half-time radio job became full time. As it happened, the University was six months away from having their television license. With small budgets, programming would be a challenge. The Homme offer was well received.

"Friendly was a much loved figure in my family home growing up. He had a wonderful gentleness about him and what is of paramount importance to me, he never talked down to the children in his audience. He always seemed to respect his viewers and that wonderful easy-going charm worked as well in relating to the adults who might be watching it with the little ones. Add to this that Friendly had books, music and Rusty and Jerome and I was hooked for life. To this day if I am channel hopping and come across an episode of The Friendly Giant I allow myself a fifteen minute indulgence of happy nostalgia. The show has worn well.

It is perhaps interesting to note that when I was creating the character of 'Holly Higgins' on Under The Umbrella Tree it was very important to me that she should have a gentleness and respect for her audience and the characters around her – certainly characteristics well documented over the years by Bob Homme."

Holly Larocque, "Holly" in Under The Umbrella Tree

8

The Giant Comes to Life

Working full time in the day on radio, Bob spent his evenings for the next six months developing a children's television show. As the medium of television was still in its infancy, everyone was learning all the time. The show was wet cement and it was up to Bob to make it smooth and durable. But what would work?

The earliest experiments with the camera did not look right. It was obviously just a person walking around a miniature set – Godzilla style. The person looked normal and the scenes looked miniature. Bob was willing to think outside the box to find what would work.

Then it struck. Eureka! Instead of the normal camera angles, raise the miniatures to camera height and place the human being as the unusual shot above the set. Suddenly, the person became the giant. Using a tight cover-shot and a loose close-up seemed to violate the newly established rules of television but it worked perfectly in creating the sense of a large giant. Part of the genius of this is that Friendly was never quite all in the shot unless it was in the music room where wide angles were necessary. Only a giant could not fit into a camera shot where everyone else clearly did.

With only two cameras and limited space, the use of the camera was critical. Bob made an early decision to never leave the viewer. Friendly was always there. Create a smooth and seamless experience was the plan. The audience should not be jarred. Those unseen and underlying guiding principles very much created the look and feel of the show that we now take for granted.

Content became an early question. Having visiting entertainers as guests was the industry standard. But with a small budget it was clear that arranging and producing that many variables would not work well in this context. It would also ruin Bob's monopoly on the giant business, if other human giants also showed up to be with him on the screen. So he took the show in a different direction.

One of his remarkable achievements was how effectively Bob eliminated the "fourth wall" of the television set. His viewers were right there in the castle. Few today in television have done this successfully even with all the available special effects and digital illusions.

Unlike many of the children's shows of the time or our era, Bob understood the relationship he had with the viewer. While many of the early shows on television assumed that the children were part of a crowd watching in some kind of circus atmosphere, Bob visualized the intimacy of a family room. Here, there would be no crowds.

Just as in radio days, there may be millions who were tuned in Bob understood that each was there very much one at a time. Perhaps it would be one, two or three children sitting watching their set. This insight also led to the idea of using chairs in miniature.

What was needed was a sense of being together comfortably with a pace that was predictable and not threatening. He also assumed that his young viewers might not make it to the television (or have the antennae right) just as the show began. So repetition would help the latecomers not be lost and it would assist the children already set to begin. This repetition or "reiteration" as it is currently called, is now recognized as a sound educational principle.

As the new venture took shape, it was clear that the pattern would be very much how Bob was himself rather than the creation of a characterization. Rather than a "fe-fi-fo-fum" giant he would be an "oh-my-ho-hum" giant. Taking what is usually associated as a scary character and making it nice makes it doubly nice. Casper the Friendly Ghost is all the more friendly because that is not how ghosts are imagined. A friendly giant therefore becomes an even more friendly giant when compared to the Jack and the Beanstalk variety giant.

"My brother and I would race in to watch the Friendly Giant and we'd often repeat in chorus, 'Look up – way up!' We sat cross legged on the floor, and didn't move through the whole show!"

Honourable Sandra Pupatello, Minister of Industry & Economic Development and Women's Issues for Ontario

---

9

The Castle Family

The first decision for Bob was to determine what other characters would inhabit the castle. The idea of a giraffe fit well. As a tall beast, it would make sense that a giraffe could visit through the castle window and talk to the giant. So the order went out to a student sculptor to create a life-size giraffe head in plaster. From the cast, a paper mache version would be made. It was to be a young giraffe with the appropriate short horns. The air date was approaching quickly and the giraffe was not quite ready.

Then catastrophe struck.

There was a flood in the sculptor's basement studio. Poor Jerome version 1.0 dissolved into a muddy puddle. The Friendly Giant would have to begin life on air on WHA in Madison, Wisconsin without a giraffe!

It is easier to imagine a children's program when you have children. A major motivation for Bob in choosing and enjoying children's television came with the birth of his own children. The early links with his own offspring were very informative and encouraging for Bob in his work.

The Homme's eldest son, Richard, had a small puppet. It was a rooster and Richard called him Rusty, a suitably alliterative name for a rooster after all. Rusty was drafted into service. This puppet would go on to be a friend of many children as well as Richard's over the years. Esther ensured that Rusty was always in his distinctive red polka dot shirt. Little did she realize then that her role as official tailor to the young rooster would continue over three decades.

Now the problem was how to use this small rooster in the large castle setting. The window ledge seemed a somewhat overpowering size for the feathered friend.

A different prop then took on a new purpose. The book bag, originally intended merely to hold the book of the day, could be more. Bob made a hole in the wall behind the bag and gave Rusty an unusual home. Little did they realize then the myriad of items that would eventually come out of that bag. Even the kitchen sink popped out on one occasion! This was a parallel concept to Mary Poppin's carpet bag where all manner of things could be found later made famous in the movies by Julie Andrews.

Every program needs a good theme song. It should be simple, attractive and suited to the nature of the show. Faced with a television program set in a castle, Bob looked for an old folk song suggesting a medieval setting and feel. With his many years of music programming and a bit of luck, Bob hit on "Early One Morning."

Bob's earlier experience with his radio show on WHA in Madison, "Just For Fun" had used a bright arrangement of a nursery tune at the opening. A slower, more final sounding version of the same tune came at the close. It worked very well.

He remembered Early One Morning had been recorded in a bright and lively mood by The Bob Farnon Orchestra for the opening. A symphonic arrangement by Percy Grainger ended with an air of great and somber finality. It was just right for the closing of the program. In Wisconsin, the recorded music opened and closed each episode.

Later, when the show moved to Canada the CBC had a rule against using a recorded theme on a program with other live music. After experimenting with a small chamber group – a very costly approach – Friendly began playing the theme himself.

Early One Morning was performed on the recorder by Friendly and accompanied by Rusty on the harp. The rooster could immediately play it as well as a virtuoso. He was quite a remarkable character.

There had been discussions about whether to have other giant visitors or a giant wife for Friendly but the decision to have an intimate relationship with the viewers made this the wrong choice for Bob so there never were other giants in the show.

Piece by piece the show was starting to come together. But there was much to do in the short six months before the show was to go to air. There were still some major gaps to fill.

"I have many fond moments of watching Friendly Giant early in the morning before the rest of my family woke up; not only was it great entertainment but it gave me a sense of security and calmness."

Marlene Corey, Television Producer

10

Rusty & Jerome Come To Life

S o it was on the air with just Rusty and Friendly. A scene designer, Dick Bolden, volunteered to become Rusty's energy source and voice. Dick was effective with the ad lib style that the show demanded. His easy manner made him a welcome addition to the team.

Bob always wrote an outline but did not use a script. This meant no rehearsal, just a review of the ideas in the dressing room. The informality and easy conversation were important ingredients for the children's comfort with being in a real chat rather than a heavily rehearsed performance.

The continuing influence of radio was clearly present in the show. The repartee of the performers was very much in the tradition of the old radio shows. Among Bob's old time favourites was the show "Vic and Sade." In that program, two or three principal actors carried the show. It was a simple show with very much a slice of life approach to comedy. It was good nonsense that had fun without putting others down. Uncle Fletcher was Bob's favourite character on the show. George Burns and Gracie Allan or The Easy Aces were other pairs who worked effectively together. All were part of the influence on Bob's style and suited his personality and remarkable sense of minimalist drama.

But what happened to poor Jerome?

Finally Jerome was rebuilt but was still not ready for prime time. The show was already on the air with Rusty but the first Jerome had some real problems as well as the need for some cosmetic surgery.

The first problem was that his ears were too rigid. That would take away a natural look and would invite a disaster on what was then live television as he might come through the window and lose an ear on the turn – a disconcerting thought for small children who would be watching. The neck also lacked the "giraffe" look. It had been made with a number of eight inch metal rings spaced about four inches apart and covered with cloth. Missing was that lithe, muscular look of a graceful giraffe. It looked more like a dragon's neck.

Esther was again the mother of invention this time. She made a tube eight inches in diameter and thirty inches long from a salmon pink beach towel. She stiffened this with buckram. When this was cemented to Jerome's head and finished with dark blue giraffe-type markings, the result was perfect. Now only the ears remained a problem.

Bob performed surgery using a hacksaw and removed the ears. Then looking at several pictures of giraffes, he created those ears Jerome still enjoys all these years later. They are made of cork, window screen, terry cloth and velvet. They will bend and quiver in a very lifelike manner. Jerome was perfect and now ready for the castle.

Of course to us looking back at our memories of the show, it is impossible to imagine Friendly and the castle without Rusty and Jerome. It was very interesting to learn how serendipitous so many of these and other pieces of the show evolved into something which seems so obvious and dependable now with the hindsight of so many years of this television institution in the United States and Canada.

It is also surprising to many of the viewers who were not exposed to the classic old radio shows and the ability of the spoken word to enchant and transport the listener without the benefit of the special effects that are part of our television and movie experiences today. The viewer and the listener had to respond to the story to the extent that they would suspend their disbelief. This involved both the quality of the production and the quality of performers. Bob and his partners achieved that goal and took us to the world of "Once Upon A Time."

Friendly's Kids –
All Grown Up – And Yet...

"I recall watching as a kid in the early sixties, when we had two, maybe three TV stations via the aerial and a black and white TV. Friendly was a Canadian institution. I remember that warm welcome and especially being offered the rocking chair by the fireplace. Our creative imaginations immensely enjoyed the fifteen minutes in what seemed like a far away land – the land of The Friendly Giant."

C. Glenn Rogers IBM Canada Software

11

Jerome & Big Ten Football

B
ut who would give this puppet a life and personality? The answer came again from Bob's varied radio experiences. At one stage of those radio days, Bob was responsible for a quarter hour of recorded marches – a rousing wake-up for early morning listeners. Bob had written several humorous sketches for station staff functions and the program director suggested that he turn out this kind of material for the march program.

Bob's closest friend at the station was Ken Ohst, chief announcer, play by play broadcaster of Wisconsin's Big Ten football games among many other things. He and Bob shared the same kind of dry humour and had often ad libbed those humorous sketches. The two of them became the entire cast of The Bandwagon Program.

Each program consisted of four short marches interspersed with an interview with one of the faculty of the "Bandwagon Correspondence School." It was one of the few correspondence schools that boasted a full-fledged campus complete with ivy-covered walls, hallowed halls, a board of regents, a president, professors, assistant professors, instructors, assistant instructors, and, of course, students.

If anyone asked why a correspondence school needed a campus, it was explained that the campus was established many years earlier during a prolonged postal strike (pa...dum!). This threatened to flunk out the entire student body, coming as it did near final exams. Ken played all of the faculty members one at a time.

There was "Dr. Russell Grouse," head of the ornithological department and chief bird-watcher. "Dr. Winston Vane" was chief of meteorology. Many more distinguished characters made up the school. A typical program would have Bob interviewing Dr. Vane on the occasion of some dense fog. The repartee was easy. That combination made Ken Bob's first choice to be Jerome.

Meanwhile, Dick Bolden was thoroughly involved with his part as Rusty. When Ken turned up at his first rehearsal with Jerome on his arm, Bolden promptly quit. He felt that this little puppet would be completely upstaged by the towering giraffe. He no longer wanted to be part of it.

The crisis was solved when the program director, who had some respect for Dick as an artist, offered him the opportunity to develop his own programs with puppets of his own design. Dick jumped at the chance. Bob put Rusty on the shelf temporarily and Jerome made his debut. The giraffe was an immediate success. Bob's instincts had once again proven true.

A year later, Bolden had taken his own show off to another station. Ken slipped Rusty on his other hand and he became a dual personality equipped with the two distinct voices. There had been an occasional test of using a third person but as with any conversation ad libbing becomes much more difficult when there are three vs. two. While there were ultimately three speaking characters there were only two performers doing the ad lib. This turned out to be a very important insight. Similarly, Bob's decision to outline the shows rather than script them was also a critical element of the successful and natural ad lib.

The program in the United States was an evening production with the young audience close to bed time when it was on air. Bob believed the idea of a friendly and quiet visit with a story or song before bed was appealing. A moon rising behind the darkened castle added a sense of closure for the day. Parents reported that the children settled well after the show.

In the early days in Wisconsin, the skeleton crew all pitched in wherever needed. This was true for Ken as well. As Friendly was speaking over the opening shot, Ken was behind the castle ready to pull the strings that lowered the drawbridge and opened the doors. Having done that, he scrambled behind the castle wall, slipped both puppets on and was ready to greet Friendly after everyone looked up.

Then after the good-byes and Friendly's hand slowly going down to rearrange the little chairs, Ken was again behind the castle. This time he would be on a stepladder and pulled the strings that closed the doors and raised the drawbridge. Then came the challenge of raising the moon by a string and the stick with two strings that held the cow. It was amazing how slow and graceful that leap over the moon could be – although they had a number of memorable occasions where moon and cow collided. In the early days, they also experimented with some paper characters like the dish running away with the spoon over the drawbridge. One of the most unexpected events was when Curious George parachuted in at the end. Whether out of the preference of simplicity or the risk of crew catastrophes while running around on the live show, only the moon and the cow would continue.

Ken was invaluable to the beginnings of The Friendly Giant. He and Bob remained close friends until Ken's untimely death.

"The Friendly Giant was a wonderful part of my childhood. Our generation was drawn into his miniature world of furniture, with a special chair for 'two to curl up in'. The hooks of the show will forever be in my thoughts, 'Wait I'll call Jerome' (whistle ... wait ... whistle #2 ... off key response from Jerome). Friendly's music was excellent, semi- classical and soothing, the pace of the show was comfortable and as the draw bridge was let down to the strains of 'Early One Morning' there was the anticipation of the next visit. I always loved the part at the end when he would pull up the rocking chair in front of the fireplace. It was as if he was putting it there just for me."

Monica Morin, Windsor Ontario

12

A Friendly Philosophy

A developing Homme philosophy was now being articulated through choices made on the show. Along with some of the creative decisions, Bob was vitally concerned with the educational impact of the program. While the show did not have an educational mandate per se, he knew that young children are always in a learning mode. He took that responsibility and opportunity very seriously. It was yet another reflection of the respect that Bob had and showed for his audience.

At this point, the show was on the NET (National Educational Television), the forerunner of PBS (Public Broadcasting Service). It was broadcast in eleven major markets throughout the country. The relationship with NET continued for fourteen years until 1968. Sadly for the American viewers, they never saw Jerome in colour – just in the black and white versions.

Ironically, when Bob was the judge in 1968 for the children's category for the NET awards, he selected a relative newcomer for the prize. Rather than any of the elaborate and well-funded projects offered, Bob was drawn to a new program. It was called, "The Muppets On Puppets" with a young man named Jim Henson. The launch of Sesame Street began that same year and NET ended their tradition of fifteen minute shows such as The Friendly Giant.

Bob was awarded the Individual Achievement award. In his acceptance speech, he pointed to the fact that there were no individuals in this kind of success – just members of a team. Bob spoke often and strongly about how important each person from the performers like Ken Ohst, Rod Coneybeare and the Keoghs to the many fine musicians like John Duncan and others to the longtime producer-director John Ryan and the production team.

Producers at the CBC included Michael Spivak (1958-59), Dan McCarthy (1959-60), Doug Davidson (1960-65), Ed Mercel (1965-66), Hedley Read (1966-71), Graham Doyle (1971-74), Gloria White (1974-75), Barry Cranston (1975-76), and John Ryan (1976-84).

Over the years The Friendly Giant program and Bob received awards from the Children's Broadcast Institute of Canada, the Ohio State Award, The Liberty Magazine Award and the Ryerson Fellowship. In its citation, the Ryerson committee said the award was "rooted in our conviction that The Friendly Giant program's elegance, gentleness and its uncompromising commitment to its audience of preschool children reflect the highest possible standard of integrity in children's television programming. It is your work as creator, writer and principal performer that we wish to recognize."

The peer and professional recognition Bob received reflected his underlying philosophy of education and the needs of children. Many teachers and performers talked down to children. Bob's chief interest in children began with his own offspring.

Most effective communication principles with children are the same as those used when working with adults. There were some obvious differences like the length of words and using simplistic concepts. In reading about developmental psychology, Bob used what was understood at that time.

The initial audience was thought to be in the three to five year old range. Bob began by making the content appropriate to the youngest of his audience. But in doing so, he became concerned about the older children losing interest. He decided to aim higher and focused on the four to six year olds.

Bob concluded that the three year olds were not bothered by things that they don't understand completely since they do not understand much at that point. They generally tag along and pick up what they can. In a sense, they are used to it. Subtle repetition and familiar contexts for new things made the ideas easy to digest.

A key idea was that he would create a stretching experience rather than appeal to the lowest common denominator and bore the older children. Treating the children with respect included not talking to them as if they did not know something obvious. To suggest that, "This is an apple – it is round and red." would not go over well to the five and six year old children. This is true of adults as well. Most people find it insulting to be told something that it is understood and that they already know.

Recognizing that young children have little concept of time and geography created challenges as well. In keeping with a liberal arts approach of expanding the experiences of the children, music was drawn from many different periods. For Jerome to introduce a song from five hundred years ago would in itself not be very meaningful. But to add to that fact something like, "Did you know back then they probably did not even have peanut butter?" brought the familiar with the unknown together with some humour.

Rather than researching what children already like, Bob took an unusual approach. He looked for things that kids might like if they were exposed to them. So in his concerts, antique and chamber music could be as much a part of the children's experience as traditional familiar preschooler songs or rock music. Since there was an obvious bond of affection between the characters and by extension with the audience, risks like that could be taken. If Friendly, Jerome and Rusty enjoyed it, the children would be open to enjoy it too. The characters made it fun.

This was in spite of the fact that they may never hear that piece or even style of music again. The concerts served to expand their appreciation and horizons a little bit. While there were some pieces of music written for children, particularly those written by Mary Syme, the majority of the music was generic. The music included the range of baroque to Broadway to folk music from around the world. Concerts were usually identified in fan mail as the favourite shows though none mentioned a specific type of music. That was exactly what Bob had intended.

The five-day cycle of the shows was Mondays, Wednesdays and Fridays for books then Tuesdays and Thursdays for concerts.

As Bob owned the show and maintained the creative control, he was able to keep the show focused on what was a priority in his philosophy and plan for the kids. He also benefited at the CBC from the leadership and wisdom of Dr. Fred Rainsberry who sheltered The Friendly Giant and other excellent shows from the prying bureaucrats and self-professed experts that every organization accumulates.

The Friendly Giant as a program was much more of an auditory experience than a visual one although the visuals were effective. In both style and content, Bob assumed that the children had wonderful imaginations. If they would listen their imaginations would be engaged. He did not believe that listening was to be a passive experience. He mentored the audience to become engaged with the conversations, the books and the music – just as Friendly, Rusty and Jerome did.

In retrospect this was very usual for its time and even today. But these choices were all rooted in his healthy respect for the children in his audience.

13

Wisconsin Roots

Friends of The Friendly Giant owe a great debt to Raymond and Roselyn Homme of Stoughton, Wisconsin (about twenty miles southeast of the capital city Madison). Their child was born Robert Mandt Homme on March 8, 1919. Thirty-five years later this small boy would become The Friendly Giant. This small town of five thousand comprised mostly of Norwegian ancestry as were the Homme family. Today there are two streets with the name Homme (Homme Court and Homme Lane) in that town that in 2007 has a population of 12,755; although no Homme appears in the telephone book at present.

The ethos of the town as Bob was growing up fit very well with Garrison Keillor's mythical Lake Woebegone. There was a strong sense of community. This extended into the rural surroundings in this land of mixed farms and dairy cattle. The topography of Bob's world was very similar to that of southern Ontario. The Yahara River ran through the town that included seven churches. It was a great place for Bob and his sister to grow up.

Ray Homme was a high school teacher who taught woodworking and other vocational subjects. But his interests extended beyond the classroom. He loved performance as an actor and a singer. The school's class plays could count on his enthusiastic direction.

Being a homemaker in the real sense of making a home was the major work of Roselyn Homme. A loving home nurtured Bob to be able to appreciate what was already around him and to dream about what was not yet. A letter Bob received as Friendly asked, "Did your Dad have a great sense of humour and was your mother a charming person?" The answer to both was "yes" and the influence on Bob by both of his parents was easy to see.

Typical of the time, the family enjoyed singing together and performing for each other on a Saturday night. Relatives and neighbours each had their own acts to perform as the need (or opportunity) might arise.

Bob and his father with their vaudeville act might have been the original Bob & Ray of later radio fame except that Bob was known as Little Ray. But as with so many childhood experiences, unseen tracks were being laid that would create future lines of travel in later life.

Like all kids, Bob loved the slow, hot summers. The Yahara River carried Bob and his father's duck boat on many fishing adventures. Like many of the gifts he received during those years, he remained true to his love of fishing through his life, including his retirement years.

Growing up through the depression was not a traumatic experience for Bob. The town folk took care of each other. With everyone in the same basic economic boat, it was a time when what was in your world was what you thought was normal. As a teacher, employment for Raymond Homme was uninterrupted if not very lucrative.

It might be a surprise to learn the kind of play that was a part of the childhood of The Friendly Giant. His father made his son round-tipped wooden swords and shields in the tradition of the noble knights. It never occurred to the young knights to hit each other – just the shields that made a loud and satisfying "thwack." Many hours were spent in friendly battle as they would slap their swords on the opponent's shield like Sir Galahad of old.

His father also told many bedtime stories of the new battles of King Arthur and the Knights of The Round Table, brought up to date and given a new setting in the familiar streets of Stoughton, Wisconsin.

One battle variation was using bamboo poles as huge squirt guns. The empty farm stable of one of the families made a great place for teams to play. Those in the barn would try to neutralize the opposition by getting them wet. They would then either switch sides or sit out to dry depending on the rules of the day. These were not games of anger or animosity but rather healthy competition and imagination.

The boys gained a new appreciation of the joys of rainy days after seeing the movie All's Quiet On The Western Front. It was a dark film shot in cold and dismal weather. The friends could imitate climbing through the muddy trenches. A friend's mother would equip them with rye crisps which of course the boys knew were really hardtack rations for their day at war.

It was the father of one of Bob's boyhood friends who used to call for his son to come in for dinner using that distinctive whistle that Friendly would later imitate to summon Jerome from the fields to the castle for so many years.

"Look up – way up" is what I remember most about The Friendly Giant. I think that quote just reminds me of someone much bigger than you and I and that brings me comfort."

El Childs, Musician

14

Story & Song

Another gift from his parents was the love of books. His father liked to read stories to the children. Combined with a great sense of humour and dramatic flair, Raymond Homme communicated his enthusiasm for the world of ideas. Books continued that tradition of stories for Bob. He particularly enjoyed Rudyard Kipling. O. Henry was also a big influence although it took Bob a long time to appreciate stories that did not have an unexpected plot twist at the end.

A tonsillectomy led to Bob's first musical instrument. After the operation he received a gift from his parents. It was a cornet type of instrument with five keys and a reed. It was the first of many instruments that Bob would master over his lifetime.

The underlying values that Bob would carry with him throughout his life took root in those years. Raymond Homme was a deacon in his church and the family tried to practice their principles of life consistently. The values were modeled for Bob and they stuck.

The role of teachers was significant as well. Good teachers inspire learning. Those who loved their subjects created a love for it as well for Bob even if the subject itself would normally be of no interest to him. This was a principle later used on The Friendly Giant. Children could respond to the enthusiasm and appreciation of Rusty, Jerome and Friendly toward music unfamiliar to the audience.

First attending West Side School, Bob moved at the age of ten to Central Side School (the name still brings a chuckle). Then it was on to Stoughton High School from which he graduated in 1937. As the years have passed, the school names have changed as the town grew. Only the high school has kept its original name.

His future was at the University of Wisconsin. Beginning in a general education program, his flair for high school math directed him toward accounting. Finding college calculus taught by a totally disinterested instructor quite challenging, Bob saw a need for change. He realized that it was the inspiration of a great high school teacher that created his interest in math and that accounting was not for him.

Entering university, at that time created a choice for each student. They could take gym, join R.O.T.C. for military training or join the band. For this musician, the choice was quick and painless. He joined the clarinet section of the band.

Before registering for his junior year, Bob realized that American participation in the Second World War was not far down the road. It did not appear that he would finish his university year if he began it. He had a draft number and would not have the protection of a university deferment nor an R.O.T.C. officer's entrée into the military.

So he decided to take a job as a bank bookkeeping machine operator while he waited to be drafted. With war and the draft taking many men to service, promotions came quickly in the bank. At twenty dollars a week, Bob was making some money.

But his love of music needed expression too. He played for dance bands – sometimes for the meals he ate. Once or twice a week there would be a dance needing a musician. Occasionally a restaurant or night club would be available. It was the time of the Big Bands but Bob especially was drawn to the world of jazz.

"I do remember the draw bridge opening and closing and that the worst part of the show was the draw bridge closing marking another 23 3/4 hours until it reopened its doors."

Mike Wells, National Advertising Manager

15

A Giant War

When the war continued to heat up in Europe, Bob made a decision to join an Air National Guard in expectation of a draft that was about to be activated. His was the first and only such unit in the U.S. It was activated on June 2, 1941 and Bob was shipped out to Fort Dix for training as a private. After the bombing of Pearl Harbor, war was declared by President Roosevelt.

With the war expanding, his unit became a group. The unit was in antisubmarine warfare. With the beginning of the U.S. involvement, this area was critical. His group soon expanded to a wing. Before long, Bob found himself at the command level in New York City. He had risen rather quickly to the rank of Staff Sergeant, a rank he held for the duration of the war.

It was a long way from the small town of Stoughton to life in The Big Apple. He was billeted in a hotel near 72nd St. & Broadway. The beauty of that location was that it was near Carnegie Hall. As a soldier he could attend the concerts at no charge. He was regular enough that he eventually was ushered by the staff into a special box. Borrowing the miniature scores for upcoming concerts from a nearby music library, he followed the music as the orchestra played.

His next assignment in the service was to go to Cornell University in the Finger Lakes district of Central New York State. His task was to study

Psychology. The military was interested in training individuals who could learn to do psychological field testing and measurement. Cornell was a leader in psychology at the time.

As it turned out, the "brass" were wrong and they did not have the expected work load for people with this training in the field after all. Bob was then given the choice to transfer to do further study.

His options were New York City, San Francisco, Madison (Wisconsin) or St. Louis. Bob's third choice was Madison after New York and San Francisco.

The orders read "Madison." That was pleasant news. Surprising friends by returning to the University of Wisconsin, he pretended with one that he was AWOL. It took some convincing to confirm that he really did belong back in Madison. Bob spent almost a year on home ground before being shipped out to the South Pacific.

Finally, Bob was shipped out to Johnson's Island. The objective was a landing as part of the Pacific war. As they neared their mission target, they saw some Navy planes fly over head. They flew in formation spelling out "VJ." The war was over.

Rather than turning around however, the captain kept going and landed in Guam. There Bob met some interesting people who were en route back from the war. With his psychology background, one of Bob's assignments was to do classification for people for discharge. Among the notables that he met in this capacity was the great actor and director John Huston who was discharged by Sergeant Robert Homme.

There were some compensations for being at Guam; they had a dance band which of course Bob joined. He performed for the army and the navy. Then it was Bob's time to return home and be discharged. By New Year's Day, he was back in Wisconsin as a civilian.

After discharge it was off to university with a plan. Bob would use his credits in psychology from Cornell and make that his major. New interests had also developed in writing, theatre and music.

Due to the rivalry between Cornell and the University of Wisconsin, credits from Cornell were not respected by the psychology department at U of W. However Wisconsin's Economics department would grant credit in the area of personnel management, so it was to be Bob became an economics major.

With so many Cornell credits to be applied to his economics major requirements, Bob was able to take many elective courses of his choice. This was where he did a great deal of creative writing. Most important, he was invited by the faculty advisor to take a course called "Music in Radio" that changed his life story.

The course was taught by an old friend, a piano player from his dance band days - Don Voegeli. Don was kept out of military service by a health problem so he stayed on at the University to earn a Master's degree in music. His course involved programming classical music, writing scripts and for those interested, announcing on the radio. Bob had found something he genuinely enjoyed. While still a student he was taken on as a half-time staff member and upon graduation he stayed on with a full-time position.

Following graduation he just kept on in radio. It meant turning down an offered job in placement for a paper company in the South. One wonders how we would have all been different had Bob left the station then for a company position.

"Mornings with Friendly, Jerome, and Rusty transported me to a world of make believe that inspired creativity, generated much laughter and encouraged me to a better person. Friendly always had a place for everyone and through this biography I'm sure he'll challenge us 'Look up...way up!'"

George Alves, Immigration Consultant (and loyal fan)

16

There Is No Place Like Home ...

In the rivers of life that can take us many places, it is interesting how often good things happen at home. Perhaps there is some truth in the closing scene of "The Wizard of Oz" when Dorothy talks about looking for things no further than her picket fence. There really was no place like home for Bob when it came to finding a wife.

Bob had met Esther many years before. She was all of three years old and lived a few blocks from Bob in the neighbourhood of a cousin. As Bob would visit his cousin, he would meet this cute girl called Esther. But there was an early complication in their relationship. Esther was only three. Bob was a sophisticated seven and much more interested in older women. Still, he would see her from time to time. However, the age gap was a great matter in those younger years. She eventually seemed to catch up to a point where those years seemed a small thing. She laughed at his jokes – certainly an important quality in any great relationship.

When Bob left the army in 1945, Esther had finished university which was unusual for a woman at that time. Bob had not graduated. At that point between her degree and Bob's age and war years, he deemed them to be tied. They were married in 1947 on May 25.

In the years that followed they had four children. They are Richard, Ann, Ruth and Peter. Later Esther and Bob enjoyed their grandchildren as well.

It was way back then when he was working at the university radio show that led to his important experience with children's programming. No one wanted to do children's television in those days, including Bob Homme. With Richard now born, Bob as father had a new interest in kids. The next time he was asked to do a children's program, Bob jumped at the chance.

Like all employees of small radio stations, Bob's job involved a little bit of everything – from programming music to reading the news as well as writing bits and pieces for a variety of programs.

"Just For Fun" was a fifteen minute program crafted to talk to children as if he were there with just one child. The focus was on one subject expressed in poems, stories and music.

A key idea was to avoid the loud sounds of a studio audience with the high volumes on the microphone. It destroyed any sense of intimacy. Bob opted for a quiet setting with no studio audience. It was relationship, not excitement.

In retrospect it was a formative experience that led to the model for The Friendly Giant. In the transition to television, Bob never forgot his roots and the joys of radio.

The pond at the University of Wisconsin station was becoming too small for some of Bob's dreams for The Friendly Giant. The Homme family was growing. Within the budget constraints of the station, there was little room for additional funds for the show.

Initial inquiries with the major networks in the United States had not been fruitful to that point. What to do?

17

Go North Young Man

Then Bob received a letter from Dr. Fred Rainsberry, head of the children's department at the Canadian Broadcasting Corporation in Canada. Bob was always impressed by the fact that CBC had an entire department devoted to children's programming. This was unusual for networks of the day. The CBC was also known for its high quality people.

The letter asked if Bob would like The Friendly Giant to do a one time visit on the "Junior Magazine" program for a live Sunday afternoon. This was the premier show in children's television in Canada. The late Bruce Atridge was the producer of the show. Bob quickly agreed to come to Canada. This would be Bob's first visit to the country.

It helps if you are a giant with ambition to have a portable castle. They do not always come in that variety. But Bob's did. So The Friendly Giant packed up for a week in Toronto, Ontario.

As most Canadians already can anticipate, there was a hassle crossing the border. In the days before 9-11 the immigration and customs service in Canada could have as its primary focus how much you spent outside Canada to collect the appropriate taxes and next to ensure that no agricultural items slipped across the 49th parallel (or as in this case – Canada's deep south Windsor, Ontario a bit above the 42nd parallel). The customs officials objected to the vines on the castle walls. The minor detail was that they were not real. But in fairness, not many of the customs officers meet a giant with a castle in tow.

A week was spent preparing for the show. The show went very well and Bob had a confirmed positive impression of Canada and the CBC

Dr. Rainsberry sent a follow-up invitation and asked if Bob wanted to do thirty-nine programs on kinescope for broadcast. Wanting more certainty Bob decided to be more aggressive and asked for a contract. He was offered thirteen weeks with an option for twenty-nine more. It was a deal.

The trail to Canada was blazed by Bob. He came up in the summer of 1958 and rented a house. Esther stayed in Wisconsin, pregnant with their fourth child who was due in October. After Peter was ten days old, they packed up the station wagon with a family of four jammed in and a canoe on top. The family for that generation was now complete with Richard, Anne, Ruth and Peter together.

Off they went to the Great White North. Due to another border problem with their furniture, the Homme family ended up in The White Swan Motel in Scarborough for ten days. The Hommes ordered an Eaton's stove, table and chairs. The refrigerator came from Eddie Black, later of Black's Photography. Finally they moved into their new home and so began the Canadian adventure.

The first head of the children's department at the Canadian Broadcasting Corporation (CBC) was Dr. Fred Rainsberry. At that point, the network was in its formative stage. When Fred was invited to join the CBC in 1954, he was teaching philosophy at Michigan State University. He remained as the head of the children's department until 1966.

Moving from his birthplace of Sarnia meant being in Toronto was another world for the young Fred Rainsberry who went to the University of

Toronto. He later studied at Yale and finally Michigan State University where he earned his Ph.D.

At that point in the life of the CBC, the School of Broadcasting and the Children's Department were separate entities. Fred's task was to develop not only the programming but also the underlying philosophy of the department.

His perspectives on the CBC and all of children's broadcasting are in his book, A History Of Children's Television In English Canada 1952-1986. It is not widely available but is an excellent source of the history of this part of the Canadian experience. I greatly enjoyed meeting with Dr. Rainsberry as well.

Dr. Rainsberry became aware of The Friendly Giant program and the work of Bob Homme through his interaction with other networks including NET (now PBS). There was also their mutual involvement with the prestigious Ohio State Awards for Broadcasting.

Familiar with the program, Dr. Rainsberry recognized that The Friendly Giant was an excellent fit with the needs of CBC and with the underlying philosophy he wanted to create in his department.

Relationships with adults tended to be authority oriented traditionally. Bob's approach was unique for television because he had the ability to wait for the children's responses. It showed a special gift for understanding children by allowing them to relax and let them build a relationship. The movements of The Friendly Giant were gentle and nonthreatening to children.

Another basic approach Bob took was to treat the children as individuals while never patronizing them. The children immediately responded to this mutual respect being modeled. Equally significant, the children could enjoy him as a peer.

"I loved The Friendly Giant!!!!! What I loved and remembered was that when I was home from school sick, it was such a treat to watch because I would miss it otherwise once I hit grade one. I used to absolutely believe that he was a giant when he would put his hand into the castle and touch the chair. I totally bought into that. As a child, when I watched 'The Friendly Giant', I would lose myself in his castle. When his hand would come into the room with the fireplace and rocking chair, I absolutely believed that giants could exist."

Julie Cuthbert, Humber College Fashion Arts Instructor

18

Life at The CBC

At CBC and in Canada, The Friendly Giant was instantly welcomed as a program. Dr. Rainsberry recognized the show as a complete entity. To him it was a model of what children's programming should be. He noted that there were no negative repercussions from Bob's U.S. citizenship.

Commercial pressure was a real force within the CBC management. The competition was between shows that were geared to a very narrow, segmented audience and the mass appeal programs. As the head of the children's department, Dr. Rainsberry had to balance the pressures of the administration with his commitment to insulate the programs from unhealthy interference.

One strategy was to provide mass audience shows like the Canadian Howdy Doody while preserving the unique strengths of the department (a point of trivia here – William Shatner of Star Trek and Boston Legal fame once played the Timber Tom character on the Canadian Howdy Doody!). Dr. Rainsberry wanted children's programming to teach them things and be free from commercial pressures. Such compromises allowed the "bean-counters" to be satisfied through the more commercial projects.

The Friendly Giant program was very consistent with the way children respond to and play with each other. From Dr. Rainsberry's perspective, it was a positive way to teach children about relationships.

Philosophically, the program understood the relationship of play to creative endeavour. Friendly used visuals to create and invite the responses of children. This was key. Part of the underlying respect that the giant had with his audience was that he invited their response. This meant that the children were not docile but engaged by the program.

This is a different response than adults have. We think of a child's response as an outward action or spoken word. But for preschoolers, there are deep responses to this stimulation about their surrounding world.

A great strength was the simplicity of production. Depending heavily on dialogue, Dr. Rainsberry saw the ad libbing as both adult and playful. The music was able to create and invite responses from the children.

For his time, Bob recognized that The Friendly Giant need not be as clearly or overtly educational as many others shows were. By making the programs playful the children learned through play and relationships. This was a very positive contribution to the children's department at CBC.

Dr. Rainsberry described Bob's approach as "not doctrinaire but just being a natural at what he did." This was the intuitive genius in how The Friendly Giant show worked. Bob was very passionate about education taking place through the show. Bob recognized that the cast's power to educate was because of their playful relationship. A real asset in this mix was Bob's natural sense of how to use TV effectively.

As Dr. Rainsberry would speak to parent groups around the country he was often asked about The Friendly Giant. As the head of the children's department, Dr. Rainsberry did not have to worry about Bob or the show; he could just let him be.

An interesting side-bar is that it was Dr. Rainsberry who recruited the late Fred Rogers to come up to Canada before Fred was on camera. Prior to this he just did scripts and voiced puppets. In the two years here he developed what became Mr. Rogers' Neighborhood. He also imported the late Ernie Coombs, better known to Canadians as Mr. Dressup, at the same time. Dr. Rainsberry described Ernie as another natural person with children.

After CBC, Dr. Rainsberry went to Israel for a year to begin educational TV there. He later taught curriculum development at the Ontario Institute for Studies in Education. He summed up his life as a "great privilege of being able to do what I wanted to do." His high praise for Bob Homme was that "he personified our policy and philosophy of children's programming."

"As a child I have many fond memories of watching Rusty and Jerome and listening to the music and stories of The Friendly Giant. There was innocence in the Friendly Giant that was a wonderful part of my childhood."

Ron J. McKerlie, Corporate Chief Information Officer, Province of Ontario

---

19

Castle Life

For someone who created, wrote and owned the trademark to a program, an ongoing concern for Bob was artistic control. Being in the context of a large network might make you vulnerable to pressures to conform to some other person's idea of what your show should be. One of the strengths of The Friendly Giant was that it was a very natural expression of who Bob was and what he believed.

Production meetings were held each week to discuss all of the children's programming. This could be a tricky experience because when you gather creative people together, there are many new ideas on how to change a show. Bob was sensitive to his need to protect the continuity of the show while keeping the relationships positive. It did not take long for the trust relationship to be established in conjunction with the CBC so that Bob was free to develop his program in his way. Dr. Rainsberry played an important role of running interference.

There was great relief as Bob knew that the CBC was a safe place for his creation. There would not be too much interference from others in the network. The production meetings just gave a sense that the work was valued.

The show was often produced in Studio 2 where The National, Canada's primary news production, was also done. It is fun for those who remember watching the news in those days to imagine that "not far away" across the room from where Knowlton Nash and later Peter Mansbridge there were the castle and set of The Friendly Giant.

Dealing with the administration of the CBC was never an issue as time went on. Bob was the writer, made the schedules, performed and owned the trademark. He carefully guarded the balance between music and booked shows in the programming schedule.

One reason that the program had such staying power was that Bob knew what he wanted the show to be. From time to time others wanted to to add new edges to the approach. Bob's mission was to ensure that the show was a nice round circle. The result was a smooth and harmonious experience with none of the rough edges so often visible in children's television.

There was sometimes pressure to do it as a half-hour program. This was a much tougher change than it would appear. Bob was very concerned that it would not be as effective as the quarter hour for the children. With a standard opening and closing it was much more than twice the content to go to a half-hour format. If you were to calculate the time, it would triple the amount of unique material for each show.

This would have required bigger casts and sets. But for Bob, the bottom line was that it was not something he would do well.

Many of the directors wanted the opening to be taped. There was pressure for one standard opening. But in the way the show worked, the opening allowed for preschoolers who often arrived late to ease into the program. It was a means to get them ready to listen.

The later repetition sparked by Rusty asking "What's new?" was then followed later by a review with Jerome. By not taping a standard opening, it gave the show more freedom to lead into talking about the subject of the day. Some days it was a farm scene that might lead to a book on cows. A standard opening would lose that flexibility.

Bob fundamentally understood his strengths and respected his audience too much to step outside where he felt he could give his best performance and their best experience.

Still More Friendly Companions

"One of the powerful contributions of The Friendly Giant is modeling respect toward others. That positive attitude was modeled in how Friendly treated Rusty, Jerome and us."

Dr. G. Blair Lamb, MD Burlington, Ontario

20

Chairs And Chains

For those who grew up in the Friendly tradition, you were always invited to choose your chair. One of the questions that viewers compare was their memory of which chair they routinely chose. There was the chair for one of you, the big arm chair for two to curl up in and the rocking chair for those who like to rock. These were all small but important details that helped create the charm of those memories.

The little chairs and fireplace set were made by the same man in 1953. He had been a cabinetmaker when he suffered a heart attack. After that he began to make miniatures including a complete set of his farm as an activity. That farm became the basis of the farm scene in the openings of the program. Each of the items was beautifully crafted and detailed. All were created especially for The Friendly Giant.

When the program first aired there was no rocking chair. As the season continued it was added. But during the first year of reruns it was seen to be missing. The both observant and kind viewers mailed Bob a wide assortment of rockers for Friendly's castle thinking that something had happened to his rocker. The fireplace was included to add a sense of warmth and intimacy. It was a perfect place to gather round with your chosen chair.

The walls of the castle interior were made of vaccuform plastic to create the appearance of stone blocks. Using smaller stones at the bottom and larger ones as you went up added to the progression perspective of a giant's figure. The main room was nine feet high by twelve feet wide.

A second set angled off to a larger room with two windows known to viewers as the music room. Bob was careful as he walked between the rooms to stay in the picture for continuity. This is where Rusty's stunt double was important. Friendly would carry a second Rusty puppet between the rooms while the puppeteer moved with his Rusty behind the set. The shot was rarely cut so that the children always felt included.

The sets used in the opening such as the harbour or the farm were larger and more elaborate at the CBC and sat on a four foot wide by twelve foot long platform.

The famous boot defined the sizes. Early on, Bob assumed that a giant had to wear boots. Esther made the first costume based on pictures in old books. The boots became more important than either of them could have guessed at that point. It was from that boot that the children would be invited to "Look up – way up!"

The castle was 24" x 20". The big front doors were about 5" x 8" each. If you look carefully, you might recognize that the two chains were actually old choke chains from a dog of the Hommes' named Mert. Originally the door opened and closed with strings. Later it was motorized. The castle along with Rusty, Jerome, the costumes and other memorabilia are now at the CBC museum in Toronto.

One of the benefits of being at CBC was that there were usually about thirty people on the production floor. Everyone had a single job to do. This was in contrast to the early Wisconsin days where the opening sets were very basic. Typically it was just a sandbox with a travel poster and sometimes moss or other foliage placed on the sand.

Ultimately, there were some eleven different sets available. At CBC, the special effects department created a farm where Bob could be very specific in his requests such as asking for a windmill for that day. A challenge for the special effects crew was the speed of the cars. They had to be scaled down to suit the size of the town. Achieving a smooth movement was tough. It would lead to Friendly occasionally joking about the car with a bad engine.

"As I child I slept little (my poor parents!). My parents placed a TV with my little rocking chair in the back of the house for me in the hopes that I would not wake them and others up (3 other siblings). So each morning I would toddle down with my favourite blanket and get into my chair. I would turn on Channel 9. Sometimes I would need to wait. The screen would be blank with those stripes on it with that god-awful hum long before the days before cable and 24 hour TV. I would patiently wait until finally the screen changed and then magically the castle would appear. The Giant, Rusty and Jerome spent each morning with me as I rocked quietly and learned the lesson of the day from the Giant.

I don't have one memory per se but I do have an overwhelming impression. The show was a peaceful loving companion which was important to a child that lived in great turmoil with an alcoholic father. The Giant was a different type man for me to see and know. He was a man with great patience, wisdom, and care who never raised his voice. Even the theme song was gentle and melodic. I still hear the harp strings plucking away. I am sure children all across Canada would agree he was our trusted friend and it would take a Giant to befriend a nation of children."

Diane Sibley, Windsor Ontario

21

Tales and Tunes

B ob chose the books used in the show very carefully. The ideal book to use on TV had pictures horizontally composed allowing the maximum of picture information to come across the screen. It was also best if the ratio of text to pictures was fairly even. But of course the content was all important. Only books that mirrored the general values established by the program itself and the expanded world of the young viewers were included.

Originally, Bob bought two copies of a book, cutting one up for paste-ups in rows on large cards. Bob soon realized that this was not good television. The desire was to create a more realistic view of hands turning pages as the book was read.

An innovation a few months later was to have an emphasis on the book itself. To get beyond holding it up awkwardly, the staff created the famous book pegs on the castle wall. It made it much more like a parent reading to their child.

A key value Bob wanted to engender was a love of books and hearing them read. He picked them for their beauty, truth or humour in various combinations.

Many classic titles were read to children on the show. The first book that he read on the show was an enduring favourite of his and the audience entitled "Good Night Moon." It was written by Margaret Wise Brown with the beautiful illustrations by Clement Hurd. It had all the elements that Bob valued in a book for the show. The story was fun and engaging. It had words that sounded great. Remember some of the phrases? "Good night moon….Good night socks… Good night mush… And good night to the old lady whispering 'Hush'." This book with its great yet simple pictures still enchants young children today.

With the show being produced in Canada, a question was whether or not to speak about Canada. The way Bob handled it was to talk a little about the seasonal changes with references to being up north. There might be some contrasts made such as occasionally talking about other places like Australia. As the show was never either in production or on air in the summer, there were never any shows that featured the summer season. However if you look closely, one episode shows a Canadian nickel.

Bob had first learned to play the clarinet and saxophone. When he joined the military, he did not want to lose his very valuable clarinet so he left the instrument at home. While stationed in New York City, he went to the giant Wurlitzer store and bought two little recorders to have something to play. It was a quick instrument for others to learn so he thought that he could enjoy some duets.

The recorder is a simple and old-fashioned wind instrument. He saw a set of these recorders in a store but was not familiar with how to play them. It was only a matter of time until he mastered their medieval sounding music. The sound of the recorder – a natural for a castle – soon became an important hallmark of the show playing all genres of music.

When he returned to the radio station after the war, Bob developed more interest in the recorder. He could not know then how valuable this simple instrument would be to his future but he always sensed the recorder would be important for some reason. As The Friendly Giant was developed, Bob knew he could not have a giant in a castle playing the sax. (That was to be something a

U.S. president could later do.) As the show evolved as a concept, the recorder was a natural choice.

Of the recorders on the show, the soprano was in the key of F – a piercing and loud sound. The soprano is in C and the alto follows in F. Next is the tenor in C and the bass plays the deep notes in the key of F. There is a very soft sounding contrabass but Bob has never owned one. The loudest recorder is the smallest. In playing Early One Morning, you can hear a different recorder being played in each of the three occasions the theme is performed each episode. The first theme is bright and high with the closing being quiet and deep. Contrary to some descriptions, Bob did not play a tin whistle for the theme – it was always the recorder.

For all the children who grew up with Friendly, no matter what their age, the sound of a recorder and the soft melody of Early One Morning put them instantly back by the fireplace in the castle.

The Friendly Giant program worked so well because it was not only a great concept but it had a great cast too – from the musical beauty created by harpist John Duncan to the many visiting world-class musicians who performed their magic. In the music room the excellent puppetry of John and Linda Keogh presented the cats and raccoons. They joined the cast in 1960 and later went on to do the show "Razzle Dazzle". They often used their daughter, Nina, (as early as the age of eleven) when another hand was needed. When Linda and John retired and took their considerable talents to Mexico, they entrusted their puppets to Nina and her chosen puppeteers.

"The gentleness, the caring, the compassion, the understanding, and the spirit of friendship and fair-play are character qualities not seen in today's television role models."

Mary Lou Halliwill, Parent and Teacher

22

A Chemistry Lesson

It is difficult to imagine The Friendly Giant program without the voice and style of the amazing Rod Coneybeare – a.k.a. Rusty and Jerome.

Coming to the CBC in 1958 meant some new relationships. One that worked wonderfully was that of Bob and Rod. Their chemistry was very reminiscent of the best of old time radio.

It derived from the same basic sense of humour. This brand was not a loud slapstick comedy but a subtle tongue in cheek approach; laid-back is a good term.

The first Canadian to actually perform as Jerome was Joe Murphy. Joe was a talented performer but handling two voices and two puppets was a challenge. It became necessary for Bob to script the show with Joe's scripts pinned to the back of the set. Bob did his best to memorize what he had written – something he had never done with his old partner Ken Ohst.

The program got by but seemed shaky, especially to Bob.

It was decided to divide the roles of Rusty and Jerome between two actors with Joe continuing as Rusty. A taller puppeteer would do Jerome. That was when Rod Coneybeare was called in.

Rod had done some comedy before. He learned about an audition for the giraffe and went to an office to meet the giant. Bob reminded Rod of Dave Garroway. Entering the audition, he was sure he could not do Jerome. When it came to using the puppet during the interview, Rod put off an actual test until it could be done in front of a camera on the set. For Rod this was a strategic stall tactic.

Leaving the interview, Rod expected never to hear about the giraffe again. But Bob called his bluff. He recognized in Rod a very broad talent and that extra quality that allows something special to happen. Soon Rod was behind this wall little knowing how often he would end up there for so many years. He started moving the giraffe's mouth and it suddenly came together. Rod became Jerome. He found that even years later he could not really do it well if he were not on the set. Just looking at Jerome did not work.

The comfortable relationship between Bob and Rod was apparent to both of them immediately. This rapport was critically important for the ad lib necessary for the show to work well.

They started a little showbiz banter. Instantly, the ad lib went well together. While Rod had never used a puppet before he and Bob were on the same wave length and shared the same style of humour.

After the first season Rod was asked to do Rusty as well. He had never done falsetto much before although he had done many voices in radio. Having only two performers allowed the use of a general outline instead of scripts for the second season which Bob knew was a better method. The show took off.

From Rod's perspective, the show had a good premise that made sense. Its appeal to children was in being relaxed with a quiet humour. Rod found himself adapting to a number of both familiar and new experiences. He had no musical background but now would be singing occasionally. He also needed to change voice ranges between the two characters. Rod never had problems changing the octaves although he says that he occasionally forgot which voice he was in.

One of Bob's strengths was that he turned and looked at the camera when puppets were interacting to connect personally with the children. It created a very intimate approach. Friendly's use of his eyes and the camera were also subtle. It was obvious that he really liked kids and had a sense of where the kids were. As a style of acting, Rod observed that Bob was in the tradition of the minimalist actors.

In his role, Rod was always working from a side monitor. It is challenging to visualize Rod twisted through the book bag hole and the window with his face flat against the unseen side of the castle wall turned to the monitor. The joys of show biz!

It was tough to physically hold up Jerome for the entire the program. It took Rod a year to develop the fatigue tolerance for holding the puppet so long.

"The Friendly Giant was one show that I loved as a kid and always had to watch; I still think of that show fondly. He always made me feel warm and cozy with Rusty and Jerome."

Aliza Garshowitz-Legge, Pharmacy Administrator

23

Two Voices Learn To Dance

It helped that giraffes were more forgivable than humans. Jerome was more likely to have great laughs. The puppet's personality could be accentuated with an in-turn on one side of his lips that could create a sneer or a sweet smile. Tilting the head a certain way could make the giraffe be either boyish or a bit of a con-man.

Jerome would regularly be seen dancing off-camera which sometimes required Rod to make tap dance sounds. It was not easy to make him look like Jerome was dancing especially if an occasional ballet was planned. Friendly would frequently look out the window and comment on Jerome's graceful footwork. The Jerome that Rod performed was kind and extroverted. His egocentric instincts were usually mitigated at the last moment.

Rusty was in contrast, quite serious. For him, jokes had to be described and explained. However, he was a bookworm and gifted musician. His personality was definitely the introvert of the group. When Rusty played the guitar or harp, it was challenging for him to make the fingers work well.

Rusty learned about his world primarily in books and from inside the castle although he would venture out to see friends and in one episode arrived back at the castle window in a raincoat with rubber boots.

Jerome learned from the outside world and experiences. The coopera-
tive relationship between Jerome and Rusty came in part from their differing
sources of knowledge. Rusty would express pleasure in knowing facts. It was
not expected that kids would learn the facts but to begin to understand that
knowing facts was fun and useful. Jerome delighted in what he did in his
outdoor world.

Rusty could play guitar, mandolin, banjo, ukulele and accordion. Being a
talented rooster, he even played the guitar left handed! Jerome could play the
harmonica and even did some drawing on the show using only his mouth to
guide the marker. The airplane he drew was well done. Quite an accomplish-
ment when you think what it took for Rod Coneybeare to pull that off!

Friendly's role was often that of a friend who could help his friend sort
out their occasional misunderstandings. Jerome often wanted the spotlight but
Rusty sometimes would fight for it too. The rooster could get angry at times but
Friendly helped create balance. Rod felt that Bob created an ideal parent and
later a grandparent figure.

The giraffe's personality was very different from Rusty. Rusty practiced
acceptance of the other characters. Jerome bragged but always as a kind of put
on. Rusty was more long-suffering and helpful. But even Rusty had his moments as he would complain about riding on Jerome's neck. There were many
physical challenges in the role of puppeteer trying to create and perform two
such diverse characters with his arms and his voices.

In concept, the show never intended to solve all of the details. It was
assumed that the show could stretch the child's belief. This allowed the children
to use their imagination without filling in every little fact. The show was done in
real time which meant that you could not solve many situations with special
effects. There was no "tune in tomorrow" to see how the subject would be
resolved. Much of the energy came because the shows were performed as live
action even when they were eventually produced live to tape.

As an auditory presentation, Rod's voice for Jerome was created to have a bit of an edge on it. It was a little more halting than his normal voice with a bit of the Jimmy Stewart accentuated "R's." It was an interesting experience for Rod to see how the puppet almost possessed the puppeteer.

Rod himself was a shy and inhibited as a child. In his early life he was much more of a Rusty type. Showbiz allowed him to be more extroverted. Jerome gave him a character to hide behind and a license to be outgoing, assertive and even aggressive.

Rod Coneybeare was born in 1930 in Belleville, Ontario, east of Toronto. He later grew up in the north side of Toronto. Always a radio fan, he wanted to be one of them. The delight in recalling these shows was obvious as both Bob and Rod spoke about their joy of working together.

Following his many years on The Friendly Giant, Rod has given his time to writing fiction. He wrote some short stories and had a book recently published. He now finds himself pursuing this earlier ambition of writing as well as lending his voice talents to cartoons and elsewhere.

"The show definitely had a soft demeanor to it and taught us all valuable life lessons as youngsters. Friendly and the crew will be missed by our generation and hopefully enjoyed by the new generations to come."

Jack Kennedy, President Lifebridge Health Management

24

Giant Friends & Foes

O ne of the rewards of a long running program is the response. This is particularly true if one loves his audience as much as Bob Homme did. Scribbles would come from the target audience of little friends. Sometimes the letter would be written by parents or older siblings. The program never asked for mail but received plenty.

Bob found that one of the main groups of writers was teens. They would write about being home from school sick. Bob had hoped it was not the kind of program you outgrew. Over the years he received many confirmations that there were preschoolers of all ages. The quality of the show encouraged adults to keep watching with their children rather than leave the television as the babysitter.

A common opening line from mail was, "This is my first fan letter." or "You wouldn't believe it but I'm forty-six and still watch your show."

Over the years, there was a consistent portion of the audience who were children with learning challenges. This was because the pace never left anyone behind. The effort to make things as plain as possible paid off.

One of the joys for Friendly was teaching children how to learn to listen to music. He encouraged parents to provide their children with more than just performance opportunities with an instrument, important as this is. Learning to listen and appreciate music is a great skill to be nurtured whether it is exciting music or peaceful and quiet music.

As he watched the baby-boomers and the Generation-X children become adults and parents, Bob had some Friendly observations. He noted the tendency of parents to accept the idea that, "These are the 90s and not like when I was a kid." This is too often used as an excuse to avoid making the tough decisions of parenting. He was also disappointed with the assumption that children will kowtow to negative peer groups and that this is expected.

Parents put up with more poor behavior by children and their children's friends because after all, "these are the 90s." He believed that a greater emphasis on modeling as parents would be more positive. In general he saw too little emphasis on responsibility. Building positive relationships early on pays off.

The underlying morality of The Friendly Giant was a great strength of the program. Bob could not imagine doing something that he personally disapproved of just because it was entertaining. These values were very much rooted in his upbringing. He understood that while the show had no mandate to teach anything kids are always learning. That is an important principle for all who work with or parent children to remember, Bob believed.

Parents can teach more by showing than by preaching. They will do as their parents do whatever their parents say. The positive values of The Friendly Giant program were always implied and shown rather than explicitly stated.

Twenty-five years on CBC meant a celebration. The time had passed quickly. Including the early years in Wisconsin, The Friendly Giant was at the time the longest running children's program in television history. But some forces at CBC wanted to end the show. Opposition by some extreme and humorless feminists and a changing flavour of the CBC began to take its toll. The show became a target.

Perhaps indicative of the tenor of the CBC at the time was how the end came for the show. When it was canceled, the news came as a surprise. Bob received a phone call one morning on the set. The voice asked, "What do you think about The Friendly Giant being canceled?" The call was from a reporter on CBC radio. Bob had to say that he didn't know anything about it.

The public reaction gave the show an unusual stay of execution. But new programming was cut way back for the following year. Finally the show was to stay on the air in reruns and the cast would do four half-hour specials. The great advocates like Dr. Rainsberry were gone from the broadcast. It was sad to see how such a long and successful relationship for the CBC was handled.

The Friendly Giant program was mentioned by Members of Parliament in the House of Commons, with cartoonists and newspapers being very supportive. One man in Montreal started petitions and hundreds of signed letters. It was sent to CBC Montreal who forwarded it through the CBC Ottawa who then sent it on to Bob unopened. True to a bureaucratic stereotype, the people for whom the letters were intended never saw them.

Toward the end there was not anyone in administration who was there when Bob first came to CBC Another negative for the program was that it was not an in-house show. As it was not under their control, there was not the same connection with The Friendly Giant as with other shows. Most of the production staff at CBC worked on the show at some point in their careers. The CBC has never been the same for many reasons. The Rainsberry years produced a remarkable collection of children's television in Canada.

It is heartening to now see the CBC museum include so much of Friendly's treasures. Like so many of the other great productions in children's television of that era at CBC, Friendly is recognized as part of a truly golden era at the network.

"The Friendly Giant was a truly Canadian phenomenon who provided an excellent role model for children. He taught the importance of sharing and getting along with others, as well as an appreciation of music and stories, to his ever-faithful audience who eagerly anticipated their regular invitations to the castle to curl up in the armchair, or sit in the Giant's rocking-chair and listen to Friendly, Rusty, Jerome, Angie and Fiddle once more."

Karen J. Kendrick-Diamond, B.A., Library Branch Supervisor

25

Friendly Moments

For Bob, there were a few favourite shows that came to mind during our meetings together. The show about "Smiles" was a keeper. It included music and great interaction between the characters. Jerome often liked to get away with suggesting old tunes by saying that it was a favourite of his mother. This set included "Shadow of Your Smile" where Jerome knew only the title. All the other words were just "Te dum te dum" just as his giraffe mom had sung the lullaby to him.

Another was about a boy who played baseball every Saturday while his sister took ballet. He secretly took one ballet lesson and it helped him be a hero in baseball as he made a diving catch. Jerome said that he can't bat but he is a great catcher. Rusty got a ball and Friendly threw the ball out the castle window. Waiting for a delayed sound effect of a can falling over meant Jerome had to keep going a long way to make the catch. Often in the show it was when things went wrong that it was really fun and memorable.

Antiques were the theme of a different day. But the old apple peeler to be used did not work. Friendly turned the need to improvise a discussion on how things do not work as well when they age. "But the old peeler worked well for many years."

A giant has extra-special expectations placed upon him. For the rehearsal of one show, he broke an apple in half. Bob did this by gripping an apple in both hands and twisting it until the skin breaks and the apple snaps in two – a neat trick for a giant to do. A well-intentioned special-effects person did a small cut around the circumference of the apple for Friendly before the live show. He hoped to make it easier for the giant to snap. Friendly was unaware of this change.

When he tried to do the trick, the skin slid about leaving a very wet and slippery surface. His hands were left soaking wet with apple juice and Friendly had to ask Rusty to pass up a towel. Fortunately, the ever resourceful rooster could find a towel. Rusty had everything in that book bag!

Another of the tests of a giant's patience came in an episode where they were talking about buttons. Friendly grabbed one of the buttons on a string and started to whirl it around and around. After many spins you can pull the ends of the string tight and then the spinning button creates a small whispering sound as the air passes through the button holes. Many of us have done this low tech trick. What had worked well in preparation for the show did not work this time. Bob would spin and spin then hush the others to listen to the sound. Nothing. Still smiling, he spun the button again and again. Still nothing. Soon the clock was running out and they had to admit that sometimes the button just will not whisper. The button had lost its whisper. Out came the giant recorder and off they went to conclude the show.

As with all television production there are many unseen experiences. The floor director gave cues to the performers. After a while the show went from hand signals to clocks. The Friendly Giant always started twelve minutes to the hour for their part of the production.

One time Rod was watching Friendly through the window and got a strange look from Bob who started to move quickly to a conclusion. It turned out that Rod's clock had been thirty seconds off. After the show Rod asked, "What was the problem?" The floor director said he had clearly signaled that it was time to wrap up. Rod asked, "When?" The director answered, "Jerome was looking right at me when I signaled! OOPS!"

With that many shows over that many years, there are many stories that reflect the ups and downs of a day on the set.

"As a young boy surrounded within a confusing dysfunctional family, raised by a loving grandmother, I always became excited when Friendly challenged me to 'Find the Boot then look up – way up'. Today, after many journeys, adventures and successes, my motto and foundation of life is to never give up. Always 'Find the boot, look up, look way up.' Thank you Friendly!"

Robert Beer Director - Palladin International

26

Forever The Friendly Giant

Retirement means different things to different people. To Bob it was something of a mixed blessing. He enjoyed the independence and freedom to travel. The opportunity to indulge at will in his favourite past-times of golf and fishing as well as unlimited time with his family and friends was great. But when one has earned a living for more than three decades from doing exactly what one enjoys most in life, there is an admitted kind of emptiness when it ends. The day by day contact with a wide variety of interesting people left a gap that needed filling.

For a time Bob says that he fell into the habit of writing long and rambling letters to old friends who, of course, replied in kind. All this was very satisfying but it placed him at the keyboard of his word processor for endless hours. This was much to the distress of Esther who frequently had to chase him out of the house for a bit of exercise!

Many people collect the paintings of artist James Lumbers. His distinctive style includes a present scene with images of the past faded in the background. It could be children fishing with an image of a grandfather faded behind them with fishing rod in hand. Bob and Esther enjoyed their friendship with the artist. Bob told me that he was a model for many of these images of grandfather types in these paintings such as "Lucky Strike" and "Gone Fishing." The Springer spaniels you notice in paintings like "Old Friends" was the Homme's Molly. In one painting of a honky-tonk piano player called "Billy

Nine Fingers", Bob and Esther are one of the couples sitting at a table in the foreground. Other friends of the Lumbers are pictured in that scene as well.

In retirement, a friend invited Bob to join the Rotary Club in nearby Cobourg, Ontario. Knowing it to be a service club made up of business and professional people, he felt that he would be out of place. He had never been a joiner of any kind; however, his eyes were opened after the first meeting. These serious, hard-working people from local business seemed more real – more genuine men and women. Each Friday at the Rotary luncheon meeting their times together became a great source of laughter and wit. It was a great outlet. To boot (no giant boot pun intended) the depth and breadth of services performed locally and all over the world was impressive. The gap for Bob was filled.

A spin-off benefit for his Rotary connection was the opportunity to play his recorder and clarinet again for a live audience. Wally Reid, a fellow Rotarian had a group Time Share to entertain in local retirement homes and social clubs for the elderly. Wally played piano, guitar and ukulele. Bob often joined them in their sing-a-longs.

Bob and Wally presented a specialty act with Wally performing for Rusty. Bob always explained that Rusty would like to have flown in for the occasion, but he is a forty-year old rooster and that's no spring chicken! Rusty had carefully taught Wally all he should know to be a great stand-in. A good time was had by all – especially by Friendly.

Another place where Bob loved to perform was the Grafton Village Inn. Grafton is the small village about 12 km east of Cobourg, Ontario and near where Bob and Esther lived during their summers and ultimately in retirement. The setting of the inn was a perfect place for Bob to perform – becoming one of the reasons to reserve at the inn for brunches and special occasions. In honor of his relationship to the Grafton Village Inn and the community, The Friendly Room was dedicated to Bob.

Canada became more than just an adopted home for Bob and Esther Homme. On November 26, 1993 they became Canadian citizens. After the welcoming ceremony in a courtroom in Peterborough, Bob had a friendly (of course) chat with citizenship court Judge Geddes. Bob's enthusiasm went so far as to suggest changes in the Canadian national anthem. He told the judge that he would sing it every Friday.

> O Canada our home and chosen land
> True patriot love in all our hearts command.
> With glowing pride we see thee rise
> This Great North strong and free.
> From far and wide, O Canada
> We stand on Guard for thee.
> God keep our land glorious and free
> O Canada we stand on guard for thee
> O Canada we stand on guard for thee.

He felt that the word "chosen" better expressed his strong feeling of attachment to this land chosen by the Hommes and so many others. A bonus is a better rhyme! Who knows? Perhaps we'll have a "Friendly" revision officially declared by the Canadian Parliament!

The country of Canada, chosen by Bob and Esther Homme, gave him its highest honour. In 1998, Robert Mandt Homme was awarded The Order of Canada in recognition for his contribution to his adopted country. He was one of only 3500 individuals at that time to receive this award since its creation in 1967. It was a fitting expression of thanks to a person who has positively affected so many of its children, their parents and grandparents.

"Watching The Friendly Giant is one of my earliest television memories. I always wished I could be sitting in the rocking chair looking way, way up."

Judi Wilson, Troubadour Music

27

Good Night Friendly

It's late.

"This little chair will be waiting for one of you."

"The rocking chair for another who likes to rock."

"And a big arm chair for two more to curl up in when you come again to our castle."

It's nice to know that you have a standing invitation to visit such a comfortable place. Everyone is always welcome at the castle of The Friendly Giant.

"I'll close the big front doors and pull up the drawbridge after you're gone."

"Good-bye. Good-bye."

Darkness has descended upon the castle. A quieter and deeper version of Early One Morning ushers us out of the castle. We watch the two big front doors slowly close. The drawbridge is lifted. In a larger view we now see the sky behind the castle.

The moon rises in the sky over the castle. A familiar smile is on its face. All that remains is for the cow to jump over the moon as the music ends.

We can only wish that the Canadian preschooler cable channel, Treehouse and others around the world would include The Friendly Giant in its schedule. If ever a part of some of the best television ever produced in Canada belongs there Friendly does.

How do you measure the impact of a person's life? Making a difference in the lives of others is a truly lasting contribution. That gift has multiplied itself over and over in the case of Bob Homme. There are many people around today who are a bit more friendly than they might have been through the efforts of a giant and his team.

It was a risk for us to begin this project. Childhood memories are very precious – especially the positive ones. What would Bob Homme really be like? Would he be like The Friendly Giant that we enjoyed so much in our growing up years? Would he be one of those crusty characters who really had no use for their audience of children – it was just a job.

We are delighted to report that our childhood memories were safe. An additional dimension has now been added to our adult life. Bob and Esther Homme were as genuine and warm people as you are likely to meet. Our times together were both stimulating and enjoyable.

It was an amazing experience to hold the "big arm chair" in our hands. To see and hold Rusty and Jerome brought a strange moment of wonder as childhood and adult life connected in a tangible way. It was much like visiting your childhood home as an adult. This has been an enjoyable project for us to do.

Bob received the Order of Canada in 1998 – Canada's highest civilian honour – for his lifetime contribution to Canada. His citation read: "He is the Friendly Giant who led us with the sparkling notes of his flute into that magical world across the moat and into the castle to curl up by the fire with Rusty and Jerome. Several decades of Canadian children grew up in the warm and welcoming environment of his long-running television series that set the standard for children's educational programming. He remains an icon of childhood, an image of quiet intelligence, gentle humour and unhurried attention who treated his audience with the utmost respect. He continues to charm and delight children and seniors with live performances of music and storytelling."

Sadly, Robert Mandt Homme passed away in his sleep May 9, 2000 of prostate cancer at the age of 81. His smile, his voice and his music now live on in memory and in the over 3000 episodes he created for us.

Perhaps one of the most fitting tributes came from the Toronto Star's cartoonist Corrigan who drew a view of the castle window with a tearful Jerome and a sad Rusty beside a recorder with no Friendly to play it.

At the closing of our interviews, I asked Bob how he would like to be remembered. The wish of Friendly Giant and Bob Homme was that he be fondly remembered.

Generations of children, parents and grandparents are better because we learned from Bob how to "Look Up – Way Up!"

Thank you, Friendly!

Share your Friendly thoughts, information and memories on the publisher's website www.palantir-publishing.com. Perhaps your contribution will be included in a future update of the book!

"What I remember most about Friendly, was he was big and I thought it would be cozy to sit in his lap on the rocking chair by the fireplace while he read a book to me. That always made me want a rocking chair near a fireplace in my own home. I have the rocking chair, but no fireplace. He was a big guy, with a soft voice."

Monica Ufholz, Kingsville Ontario

Friendly On Friendly c.1984

In May of 1984 The Friendly Giant will have been on the air somewhere In the English-speaking world for thirty years making it, quite possibly, TV's longest running daily children's program. Having been interviewed a hundred times or more during the course of his thirty years as The Friendly Giant, Bob Homme has volunteered to undergo one more examination.

This, however, is an interview with a difference; for the interviewee is also the interviewer. That is to say, Mr. Homme will ask himself all the questions he has always hoped someone would ask him some day.

Since he has only himself to face, he will be able to be himself without considering whether his demeanor matches that of the TV character he plays. There is not a great deal of difference between Homme and Friendly but naturally in public and on TV he tends to be a bit more polite and moderate than in real life. In this interview he will speak plainly and to the best of his ability briefly, which for him is not easy.

Q: Mr. Homme, many of your first viewers have grown up and I'm sure would be surprised to know you are still producing programs and are on the air daily after four years at the University of Wisconsin's pioneer station WHA, and twenty-six more with the CBC across Canada.

A: That's true. Most of the letters we get nowadays come from young mothers in their twenties. They tell us how surprised they are to come across the program while looking for something suitable for their 3 year olds. They all express pleasure that it hasn't changed in all those years – same characters, same mood, same deliberate pacing.

Q: That must be gratifying.

A: It certainly is.

Q: What would you say is the secret of the program's longevity?

A: Oh, many things enter into it. For one thing, the uncomplicated format and limited number of characters make it a relatively simple show. It's easy and a lot of fun to do and I think this makes it easy and fun to watch. Of course, it's not everyone's cup of tea, but there are those who like us.

Q: Who writes the script?

A: I do, although there is no actual script. I choose the subject of each show and select the materials needed e.g. a book or music. Then I prepare a fairly detailed outline, including bits of sample dialogue, giving the general direction of the plot and suggesting appropriate attitudes to be taken. From there on we ad lib it.

Q: Do you have a chance to rehearse it several times?

A: No. We have time for just one run-through. But this is no problem. Jerome and Rusty are played by the brilliant Rod Coneybeare with whom I have been working happily for 26 years. After one run-through we know pretty much whether we have any problems to solve – to shorten this bit – lengthen that – and so on. Often we get a better show out of a rehearsal that had lots of problems. The concentration needed to solve them helps sharpen the mind. Then, too, I deliberately slow our pace which gives us time to think.

Q: I'm interested to hear that you feel problems help improve your performance.

A: I'm glad you caught that. It happens all the time. For example, here's an actual case. It's Monday morning and we are going to tape a show that features an antique picture book which is 100 years old. After reading it we are to talk about other antiques – toys, tools, clothing used 100 years ago. A week before the show I had asked for an antique apple-peeler, an antique music-box, and an antique paperweight (the kind with a snowy scene inside a glass globe). This should be interesting to look at and listen to; it might help develop a preschooler's concept of the passage of time – historical perspective. But for various reasons, we had trouble with the props. The apple-peeler wouldn't work, the paperweight turned out to be a Japanese plastic toy with Bambi inside, and there was no music-box at all. So what did we do? Well, we used the apple-peeler and showed that it didn't work, pointing out that it probably did a good job for 75 years or so – and nothing lasts forever.

Q: What about the paperweight and the music-box?

A: We substituted a couple of old songs – songs as old as that apple-peeler – and they were about old things. We played and sang "Old King Cole" and "This Old Man". It was a nice show, actually.

Q: How do you account for the inadequate or missing props?

A: Oh, that just happens sometimes – mixed signals, slight misunder-standing of what was needed, any number of reasons.

Q: And does it bother you?

A: Not in the least. It would be ridiculous to jump on the props man for it. He has undoubtedly rescued far more shows than he has flubbed. We can ask him anything at all at the last minute and he'll do it, and do it beautifully and cheerfully. For example not long ago we were asked to tape a brief Christmas greeting – just the three of us, Friendly, Rusty, and Jerome saying, "Merry Christmas and Happy New Year from our castle to yours." Just before we were about to tape it, I got a bright idea; if we had a giant wreath covering the window with the open part of the wreath covered with thin red tissue paper, Jerome could come bursting through with his greeting. It would add just the right touch of humour. But it was too late to construct such a wreath. "Not so," says the props man, Gus White, disappearing with that wild Newfoundland gleam in his eye. Ten minutes later he returned with a beautiful wreath exactly the right size backed with tissue paper. He nailed it to the castle wall over the window and warned us that the glue was still drying. We taped our bit with Jerome making a spectacular entrance as we all shouted out our greeting. Then Rusty turned to Jerome with a nice air of solicitude and asked, "Did that hurt your face?" and Jerome replied reassuringly, "No, it was fun, actually!" So our problem was solved and we got a better bit out of it thanks to Gus.

Q: You seem to be dwelling a bit on your problems.

A: Yes. I did so to make the point that it is the presence of problems, not their absence, that makes life lively. The pleasure of solving problems is what separates humans from other animals. In addition to the problems that come rushing at us naturally, we create our own. That's what games are – created problems. Art and sciences too, for that matter.

Q: You're getting pretty far a field, aren't you?

A: I like it out here.

Q: Getting back to the show, you mentioned that Rod Coneybeare has been with you for 26 years. Are their any others?

A: John Duncan, our harpist. He's another man who makes the show easy to do; therefore easy to watch and listen to. It isn't everyone who can wing a show as we do and get away with it. But John has been playing harp in Toronto since 1927, so he knows his way around the instrument very well to say the least. As a matter of fact, he built the harp he is currently playing; built it from scratch, turned the screws, made all the intricate fittings, did the woodwork, the gold leaf, everything – amazing.

Q: How about your director? Another 26 year man?

A: No, but John Ryan has been with us longer than any other director. I guess we've had more than 20 all told, some for 4 or 5 years, others less. John began in 1978, I believe, and we get along just fine. To direct our loose kind of ad-lib show requires the same kind of intuitive approach from the director that Rod and I use. The three of us have to sense what each of the other is doing at all times – just ahead of time, when possible. It is probably very hard for a director not to try to put his own distinctive stamp on a show – his way of shooting it, pacing it, his own personal style. But, if our 20 or more directors had each done that, the show would have been stamped to death years ago. John Ryan is a very patient and understanding person. Our last five years have been our best.

Q: Are you just saying that so you'll always get your own way in the future?

A: Probably.

Q: Who else is an integral part of the show?

A: The P.A.'s, that is the script assistant and the floor director known as production assistants. Marlene Lawrence is our script assistant and she is, to use an old-fashioned word, a whiz. She solves problems before anyone else knows there's one around and makes my job very easy. She has a way of correcting errors I make without calling attention to them. I thank her for this. She's nice.

Q: And the floor director?

A: That's Dennis Ouellette. Like Marlene he has a way of making difficulties disappear like oil on troubled water, infinite patience and good humour, except for his jokes. But then noone is perfect.

Q: Are there any other 26 year veterans of The Friendly Giant other than Rod Coneybeare and John Duncan?

A: Yes. There is Mary Syme, concert pianist and composer. She has been creating musical gems for piano, recorder and drums since the earliest days of our program and continues to do so with unending zest. And there is Hugh Orr, recorder virtuoso and teacher. Whenever more than one recorder is heard on the show the other one is played by Hugh. If there are two extra recorders the third is invariably played by one of Hugh's ex-pupils, who are legion. I'm not sure when Hugh began playing in our concerts but if it wasn't 26 years ago, it was close.

Q: Anyone else?

A: Well, there is one other very special person, Nina Keogh, puppeteer extraordinaire. When we have concerts she is either a Siamese cat or a raccoon. And she is great. Nina hasn't been with us for 26 years but her parents, John and Linda Keogh of the Canadian Puppet Theater, were our original puppeteers 26 years ago. Nina was just a moppet (sic) at the time. She began doing special bits for us when she was eleven. When John and Linda moved to Mexico to pursue their artistic careers, Nina took over. She handles one of the puppet musicians; the other is handled by Bob Stutt, another genius. Their rehearsals are X-Rated, but their final performances are always tastefully funny and utterly realistic.

Q: Anyone else you'd like to toast as long as you're in such an affable mood?

A: Oh, the whole crew, the technical director, the cameramen, the sound-men, the lighting crew, stagehands. They are not as close to the show as the others but we are lucky to have practically the same crew every Monday. It does make life a little difficult when too many new people turn up at once. I suppose almost every technical person on staff has done his stint on our show and very few have complained. They apparently have a good time – almost as much fun as Rod and I have. By the way, I haven't said enough about Rod. I doubt that I could. He's really an amazing performer.

Q: Thus far you seem to have liked everybody and everything about your work. Don't you ever lose your temper, wax sarcastic, speak out against something? Aren't you human?

A: I'm glad you asked that question. Ask another.

Q: In your thirty years what do you regard as your greatest achievement?

A: Surviving the Year of the Child.

Q: But such a year focused attention on children's programming. Why was that so difficult to survive?

A: Well for more than a score of years we had gone on happily enjoying the generously expressed appreciation of a substantial audience of parents and children. Then with The Year of the Child came a host of experts – self-appointed – or might I say self-anointed. Their opinions, loudly expressed in all the media, were just a little hard to stomach.

Q: You seem to have a rather negative attitude toward experts.

A: Not at all. Experts if properly trained and thoroughly schooled can be, and often are, quite harmless.

Q: I see. But the self-appointed types are not harmless, right?

A: You put that very well.

Q: But though their opinions differ from yours, I'm sure you must agree that each person has the right to hold and express an opinion.

A: True. But that notion must not be construed to mean that such opinions are necessarily equal in value to all others. Some opinions are sound, based on good judgment, taste, knowledge, a special interest in a given field and the energy to develop that interest. Other opinions may be founded chiefly to grind some personal axe, usually thought to be in the service of humanity.

Q: I seem to have touched a soft spot.

A: You bet.

Q: Let's move on to another subject.

A: Don't mind if we do.

Q: Awards.

A: Ouch!

Q: I have often heard The Friendly Giant referred to as an "award winning" program. Is that a fair description?

A: Technically I suppose. The first four years the show was awarded three firsts at Ohio State which was the only competition going at the time. A year or so later, a number of newspaper critics saw to it that Friendly was given a Sylvania Award – a very nice bronze statue of a lady with an electric clock in her tummy – by Don Ameche in person at the Plaza Hotel in New York City.

Q: That must have been exciting.

A: Oh, It was. And it was exciting returning to Toronto from New York

Q: You seem to be rather negative about this treasure.

A: Unfortunately the Customs folks decided that, although it was an award, it was dutiable; it was also a clock. I offered to rip out the cord and never use it but they were adamant and extracted $65 which was probably about four times its retail value. I wanted to leave it with them but my wife said our kids would be disappointed if I returned empty-handed.

Q: A truly heart-rending tale.

A: And worse, the clock stopped running after a month.

Q: And was that your last award?

A: Almost. A few years later the program was given the Liberty Award, the same year Liberty Magazine went to the wall. Come to think of it one hears very little about Sylvania these days. In 1968 the NET people gave me an award for individual achievement. That was odd because in a medium as complex as television, achievement is always a lot more than individual.

Q: And that's it? How about the coveted award from the Children's TV Institute?

A: Ah, yes, just a few years ago and I appreciated it as I would any act of kindness.

Q: Do I detect a suggestion of bitterness?

A: I find it awkward to discuss awards. If you win one and talk about it you come off a braggart; if you fail to win one and pretend to be unconcerned, one suspects a sour-grapes attitude.

Q: Well, then let's not talk about awards anymore.

A: No. There are a few things I'd like to say on the subject. The first is that I have sometimes been involved in competition as a judge and other times as competitor and frankly I don' know which position is most uncomfortable. I guess what I dislike most is the notion that one program can honestly be said to be "the best" in any given year.

Q: Why?

A: Because within each category there is such a mixture of program types. Some are once only specials, some are purely educational, others purely entertaining, and then there are the modest, every day, bread and butter programs like ours.

Q: I think I see what you mean. To choose the so-called best from such a mix is like comparing apples and oranges and that's a problem.

A: I used to think that, but I've changed my mind. It is like comparing apples and oranges, but there is nothing really wrong with that. To some degree all comparisons are of that nature. What bothers me is something else and I've never had much luck expressing it.

Q: Go ahead. Try once more.

A: Thank you. The way to choose the best of a mixture of apples and oranges is to examine each one carefully, comparing the apples with an ideal apple and the oranges with an ideal orange. Then if you feel you've found a world-class apple and only a run-of-the-mill orange, the apple wins. Is that clear?

Q: Perfectly.

A: Actually, I don' think so. There is another angle that needs to be considered. Remember that theoretical expert I mentioned, the one with the personal axe to grind?

Q: I do.

A: Well, let's say that expert is our judge and that expert happens to be a big orange person, loves them firmly, believes they are the greatest thing in the world – lots of vitamins, beautiful color, delicious flavour and so on – but couldn't care less about apples. Such a judge will pass up the world-class apple in favour of the run-of-the-mill orange every time.

Q: That's a juicy metaphor but could you be a bit more concrete?

A: I think so. What I'm getting at is that judges ought not to be in the business of making awards based chiefly on what might be called the message value of a program instead of on its artistic values, its success at accomplishing what it sets out to do, its originality, its style.

Q: But surely content counts for something.

A: Of course it does. But, I think it must be assumed that the very act of nominating a program assures us that it has adequate positive values. And from that point on the focus should be on how well the program does – what it sets out to do.

Q: You said that before.

A: And I'll say it again.

Q: Since you seem to be getting a bit testy, let's move on to another subject – your choice.

A: There is something I'd like to bring up and in a way it is the same subject – awards.

Q: But, but ...

A: The awards that mean the most to me are those that come not from experts, but from the audience – the children and their parents.

Q: I'd like to thank you for this interview. It was fun.

A: You mean we're through? That's all?

Q: You'd like to continue?

A: Yes. There are so many questions I'm usually asked that you haven't touched on.

Q: But I thought the idea was to ask questions you have not been asked a thousand times.

A: True. But since certain questions come up so often it might be a good idea to answer them thoroughly once and for all. For example, ask me why the show is only 15 minutes long.

Q: Alright why is the show only 15 minutes long?

A: The show is fifteen minutes long because it wouldn't work as well if it were longer. Each program begins with a prologue introducing the subject of the day as we stroll along one of the miniature sets – the farm, the village, the pond, any of a dozen scenes. Then, inside the castle, the subject is introduced to Rusty and Jerome. Then follows either a book on the chosen theme or a concert somehow related to the same idea. After this there is what might be called an epilogue or summing up – some little original bit involving the three of us – also related to a chosen subject. Then the good-bye music. Each segment lasts just a few minutes. Our aim is to achieve a sense of unity and at the close a feeling of finality, as though there is nothing left to say today on this topic.

Q: Have you ever tried to expand the show to a half-hour by lengthening each segment? Slowing down a bit?

A: Yes. Years ago. It didn't work in my opinion. Slowing down from the already leisurely pace would be deadly. And lengthening the segments – say reading a longer book – is simply not good to look at on television. Our books are written for preschoolers and can be read in two or three minutes, four at the most. We tried the Dr. Seuss books which are much longer. Entertaining as they are, the business of turning that many pages became tedious. They seemed to cry out for animation. Then we tried combining a book with a concert, but such a solution is very costly.

Q: Why not break the show up into a number of short segments – maybe add some guests or other characters, and develop some new sets? It seems to me a little imagination would solve your problem.

A: What problem? I like the fifteen minute format. And if we broke the show up into shorter segments we'd lose that unitary sense I mentioned earlier – that all-of-a-piece feeling. We'd be just another cute TV show.

Q: But everyone knows that the attention span of preschoolers is very short and tying a lot of brief segments together seems to be the logical way to keep them watching.

A: Yes, everyone knows that. But what we're trying to do is help the preschooler stretch that short attention span over a longer period. That's a very necessary part of growing up. Many people don't make it and all their lives they must be spoon fed bits and pieces – a little honey with everything. That's diverting but not genuinely satisfying.

Q: You're getting a bit deep.

A: Perhaps you're right. Ask me another. Ask me why we play the music we play.

Q: Why do you play the music you play? Do you research it to see if what you play appeals to children? Why don't you play rock music? Why ...

A: Hold it! I'll answer your questions in reverse order. We don't play rock music for a number of reasons; one, there's no shortage of it. In fact it's hard to avoid. Two, we don't play rock for the same reason we don't read comic books.

Q: Just a minute! You're going to offend a lot of people with a remark like that.

A: I guess you're right and I apologize to all the comic book fans. Your second question was, "Do we research our music to see if it appeals to preschoolers?" The answer is "no." We are less interested in discovering what they like at the moment than instead of discovering what they might like if given a chance. We want our audience to sample as much as possible of the world's music. Within the past year we have played Handel, Haydn, Bach, Telemann, Frescobaldi, Gibbons, Palestrina, Purcell to name a few. Also, Cole Porter, Rodgers & Hart, Jimmy Van Heusen, Frank Loesser, Hoagie Carmichael, and many more. In addition we have sampled folk music from the U.S., Canada, England, Scotland, Ireland, Wales, Norway, Sweden, Denmark, France, Germany, Italy. Plus original music written for us by a number of Canadians – notably pianist-composer Mary Syme who I mentioned before as one of our 26 year people.

Q: What kind of music seems to be most popular with your audience?

A: That's an interesting question with an interesting answer. Almost every letter we get states that the concert programs are the favourites, but in 30 years not one viewer has ever specified which kind of concert was preferred. And that is just exactly what we want. I'm very pleased with that.

Q: Of course music has always been popular with kids. They love their little songs.

A: Ah, but these are not songs. Our music is about 90% instrumental. And most of the songs we do use are not the kind children will sing. We do not try to teach little songs.

Q: What do you have against singing?

A: Nothing. I love it. But again, there is no shortage of children's songs. Almost all children's records are vocals – sing-along type – and many children's TV programs do a good job of teaching songs. But listening is an art, too, and that's what we have chosen to encourage. I do not regard listening as passive. When I see a child with a distant, dreamy look as the music is playing I like to think that the child is not bored or disinterested but simply enthralled. Sometimes I'm right.

Q: Well, that just about takes care of music. What about books?

A: I love books. Always have. But we do have some special problems with books owing to the limitations of TV. There are many excellent books which we simply cannot use because they would not be effective on the screen. One of the most common problems is an uneven mix of words and pictures resulting in the need to stay on one picture a very long time, then skipping quickly over the next few. Somehow this is more irritating on TV than when seen by a child while sitting in a parent's lap. Also, many very beautifully illustrated books may not come across on TV simply because their composition is vertical rather than horizontal and they do not fill the screen without losing a great deal at the top or bottom. This is not fair to the illustrator or the viewer. And there are many other difficulties. I mention this to account for the fact that many of our viewers' favourite books may never be seen on our program and they may have wondered why.

Q: What do you look for in a book?

A: In a book I look for truth, beauty and/or humour or any combination of the above. A book about things a child is familiar with is good. Also, books about something totally new and strange. Any book that helps lead youngsters outward to the world as they will know it sooner or later is a help. Stories are good; adventures with surprise endings or endings that turn out just as one expected – they're fine. Any book well conceived and executed by that marvelous combination of author and illustrator is worth reading. Those books put together by that equally marvelous combination – the one person author-illustrator – are often the very best. Big books are fun. So are very small books. And poetry – there's not really enough poetry in the world.

Q: If you like books so much what are you doing on TV?

A: Reading books. Next question.

Q: Apart from introducing children to books and music, do you have any other purpose in mind when you do a show?

A: Yes. We want to show by our enthusiasm that life is full of pleasure and profit if you keep your eyes and ears open. We are not aiming at direct teaching of any given subject. For example, if Rusty regales us with a list of facts and figures about mice – -how many there are to an acre, how much grain they eat in a week – we do not expect our preschoolers to understand or remember it all. But, we hope that the general notion that it is fun to learn such things will come across as Friendly and Jerome express amazement at Rusty's erudition and Rusty bursts a bit with pride – albeit modestly.

Q: Interesting. This has been enjoyable and I suppose you could go on and on. I know I could.

A: I'm sure of it. We both know there is so much to say after thirty years; so many fine people from the earliest years. We haven't even talked about Ken Ohst, the first Jerome and Ed Sprague, our first director and so many others. But this has been a long interview and everything must come to an end I suppose.

Q: I suppose so. How about The Friendly Giant? Any end in sight?

A: Let's talk about that some other time – maybe next year.

Q: I'm willing to wait.

A: Somehow I knew you would be.

Q: Say good-bye, Friendly – the way you always do.

A: Well, it is late. This little chair will be waiting for one of you and a bigger one for two more to curl up in and a rocking-chair in the middle for someone who likes to rock. I'll close the big front doors and pull up the draw-bridge after you've gone. Good-bye, good-bye.

The Friendly Giant was a part of my sons' lives when they were growing up. As a mother, I knew there would not be anything objectionable on the program. I could safely 'park' the boys in front of the TV and try to get some of the many tasks taken care of that go along with a big family of four boys!

Mrs. Winifred Lynn, Windsor Ontario

29

A Friendly Speech – Typical of His Talks With Seniors c.1994

Afternoon. So good to be here to say a few words to an audience of my peers – seniors, that is. I'm in my 75th year and enjoying it immensely. I feel a bit misplaced in this role since for at least 40 years of my 75 I have spent the bulk of my time addressing the very young children in grades 3 to 5 for a few years on radio and the rest of the time talking on TV to preschoolers and perhaps a few teenagers home from school with chicken-pox, sprained ankles, measles – things like that, who look back at their own preschool years of watching the Friendly Giant with great nostalgia – you know, the good old days.

One might think that there is a great gap between addressing the very young and appearing before people our age. I haven't found it so. For the most part I talk the same way to the youngest as to the oldest. The same tone of voice, the same pace (which in my case) is rather leisurely, and with as much clarity as I can command.

Of course, with the very young, one must take into consideration certain concepts that at an early age have little meaning. Such things as historical time, geographical space and the countless experiences that occur only in the world outside the family setting, the home, and are therefore unknown and puzzling to a three year old – something to be approached carefully.

When I first began I was acutely aware of these limitations and we made a great effort to speak only in the simplest terms, short words, short sentences, exaggerated slow pace, and stories dealing only with experiences common to the very young.

As you can guess this made for a better show for the one and a half to three year old audience, but a pretty dull show for fours to sixes. After thinking it over we came to the conclusion that the program would be more effective if instead of aiming at the youngest, hoping the 4 to 6s would hang around, we aimed primarily at the 4 to 6s and count on the 1 to 3s to tag along.

My inspiration for this deep insight was a humorous story about an Ontario lady visiting Cape Breton who watched a Maritime lady dropping lobsters into a pot of boiling water, "Oh, doesn't that hurt them?" asked the Ontario lady. "Nonsense," said her Cape Breton friend. "We've been doing it for years – they're used to it!"

I know that's a rather cruel story but it does make the point. The very young are dropped into pots of incomprehensible adult voices for hours at a time – they're used to it. And they're luckier than the lobsters; they quite literally will grow to enjoy it.

The stuff of which our show was made was mainly words, music, and pictures – stories, poems, picture books, songs and instrumental music. What we looked for in a book was truth, beauty and humour or any combination of those qualities. In music the door was wide open. We wanted our audience to sample as much as possible of the world's music – not what someone has decided as THIS generation's music. In any given year we would have played Handel, Haydn, Bach, Telemann, Frescobaldi, Gibbons, Palestrina, Purcell – to name a few. Also Cole Porter, Rodgers and Hart, Jimmy Van Heusen, Frank Loesser, Hoagie Carmichael and many more. In addition we have sampled folk music from the U.S., Canada, England, Scotland, Ireland, Wales, Germany, Italy, and so on – plus original music created for us by a number of Canadian composers.

And this music along with the hundreds of picture books and poems were all strung together by dialogue or I suppose trialogue between a giant, a giraffe, and a rooster.

You'd probably like to meet Rusty and Jerome. I brought them along. They enjoy an afternoon out once in a while.

Here's Jerome. He doesn't look a day older than when he did the day he was created. Of course he used to get a new neck every few months. I didn't. There's a kind of trigger mechanism inside to move his jaw. "Hello, Friendly! Hey what's happened to my voice – I sound like you!."

And this is Rusty (falsetto). I can do his voice pretty well. A falsetto is a falsetto. Rusty almost always wore a polka-dot shirt. My wife, Esther, must have made at least a hundred of them in the thirty-two years we were on the air.

These two puppets were both manipulated and voiced by one man, Rod Coneybeare without whom life in the castle would have been pretty dull.

Each program centered around a single theme. The themes were sometimes those familiar to a young audience or, as often something fresh and new, but something that would eventually become familiar. There was a reason for holding to a single, central idea for each program. Everyone knows that the attention span of a preschooler is limited. Almost everyone in the television programming business knew this and adjusted to it by breaking up programs into little bite size pieces. This was a clever way of holding attention especially over an hour or more of viewing.

Our idea at the outset was not to adjust to the short attention span, but to stretch that attention span. That's an important part of growing up. That is why we held the program length to a quarter of an hour.

Fifteen minutes is quite a long time to hold the attention of a preschooler. We tried to do it by using a comfortable opening ritual during which the giant spoke directly to the audience as the camera trucked along an exterior miniature set – a farm, a harbor, a train station, a city – almost any thing that would show what the subject of the day was to be.

Then there was the invitation to choose a chair in the castle – one small chair for one of you, a bigger chair for two or more to curl up in and for someone who likes to rock, a rocking chair in the middle. Then we look up and called Rusty. Friendly repeated what he had been talking about over the opening miniature set earlier – this time to Rusty. When Jerome arrived, Friendly and Rusty broke the news to him. By this time our audience, including the late-tuners in and the restless, had a good idea of what to expect. They'd heard it three times.

This was our usual opening, the beginning of the show.

The middle was either a picture book or a concert – the subject of the book or concert being the one described in the opening. The concert was usually instrumental but sometimes included songs. The reason for leaning on instrumental music in preference to songs was simply that there is a scarcity of instrumental music offered to the very young and a great deal of singing in which the audience is invited to participate. I am not opposed to this but I do feel that simply listening is a valuable talent to cultivate and it is one almost always ignored in conventional programming.

When the concert is over or the book read to its end we slow down and sum up the whole thing. We take our time about this and never ever, ever shout out to the audience, "Hey kids, that's all we have time for. Sorry about that. We'll be looking for you tomorrow for more fun and games in the old castle with crusty little Rusty and that jim-dandy joker, Jerome! Thanks for comin'. See yuh!"

Instead, we bid each other a quiet good-bye. Friendly plays the good-bye music. We look down, way down as the chairs are put back in their accustomed place ready for tomorrow and the cow jumps over the moon.

That just about describes our program which began on an educational television station at the University of Wisconsin on May 8, 1954, close to 40 years ago. National Public Radio carried it in the States from 1955 to 1968. The CBC produced it and telecast it from 1958 to 1986.

It is currently being shown twice daily as reruns in B.C., Alberta, and Saskatchewan on educational television and on cable across Canada on YTV. The CBC no longer carries it.

And now I have this opportunity to speak to an audience that may have watched The Friendly Giant with their own preschoolers and then watched it again while babysitting their grandchildren. That's what happened in our family. I was thirty-five when Friendly began. Our first child was almost four. Now we have three grandchildren of the age that might watch it. Oh, we have four more but they are a bit too old. Quite blasé, you know.

What I would like to say to you if you DID watch with your children is "Thank you!" It was our intention that you should watch. We tried to make the program as interesting and amusing for adults as we could without becoming too complicated for our target audience. We wanted the program to draw parents and children together laughing at the same things, enjoying the same stories, the same music.

Too often today's TV for children drives parents and children apart. Either the action is too frantic, the language too coarse, the music too common, for mature acceptance, but the children are allowed to watch anyway. Many parents may regret what is happening but accept it. After all, these are the nineties. They say that times change – that sort of thing.

I don't think so. Not necessarily.

I suppose these last few observations make me sound like a proper fuddy-duddy or curmudgeon to revert to slang of an earlier day.

Well, you know, I don't mind. These may be the nineties and my ideas came out of the fifties, dating back to the thirties but I really don't think I would change my approach if I were starting out today. I'd even choose the same music – like this:

(At this point, Bob would take out his wonderful clarinet and share his music with the group.)

30

The Golden Age of Children's Television In Canada

It is difficult for most of us to appreciate the enduring qualities of The Friendly Giant as a television program. Many of his viewers were watching the show for a couple of years in preschool, then occasionally through the summer re-runs or during school breaks and days home when sick. Some of us were able to introduce our children to the show as a second generation of Friendly's kids. Others may have been the parents who introduced Friendly to their children in the 50s or 60s then later with their grandchildren in the 70s or 80s.

Canada was governed by Prime Ministers Diefenbaker, Pearson, Trudeau, Clark, Turner, Mulroney, Campbell and Chrétien over the years Friendly was on the CBC. The Auto-Pact was created. The 60s saw the beginning of the Canada-wide Medicare. The new Canadian flag was unfurled for the first time. Trudeaumania came. We went through the Centennial Celebrations of 1967. The FLQ and the October Crisis would follow soon thereafter. An election in Quebec brought the separatist PQ to power. Trudeau went. Trudeau returned. Trudeau left again. We had an energy crisis, learned a new acronym – GST and we signed the Free Trade agreement with the US.

As with any area of life, quality is no accident. Many children's shows have come and gone over the same decades. Some were quite forgettable while others had a lasting impact. Here are just a few of the more significant Canadian shows that were intended for a similar audience of preschool to the primary grades.

Chez Hélène was another of the CBC children's shows. It was produced in Montreal and featured Hélène Baillargeon as the French-speaking Hélène who gave most English Canadian children their first positive experiences with French. Interacting with her in French and interpreting for us was the character Louise played by Madeleine Kronby who being bilingual could speak to both Hélène and the cute little English speaking mouse, Suzy. The program ran from 1959 until 1973. Like The Friendly Giant it assumed that learning was happening but modeled the process of learning another language by observing the relationships of the characters interacting quite naturally with each other.

Paul Sutherland created Tales of the Riverbank in 1959 that creatively used living animals such as a hamster, a white rat, a turtle, a guinea pig and others to act out the stories set on a river complete with boats, cars and houses. Hammy Hamster was the principal character and lived in an old boot. The use of the animals with the many voices gave an endearing charm to the program that ran until 1963. It reappeared in color in the early 1970s and then again in the early 1990s with the title Once Upon A Hamster. It was a very innovative program that cleverly combined the appeal of living pets with them being in places and doing things you would not expect.

Butternut Square was memorable not so much for its three years on CBC Television from 1964 to 1967 but because it included both Fred Rogers as Mr. Rogers and Ernie Coombs as Mr. Dressup who would both go on to important and durable careers in children's television in the years that would follow.

Mr. Dressup had new episodes from its beginning on CBC from 1967-1996. It continued in reruns until 2006. Ernie Coombs had a very likeable persona that communicated well with children. As with The Friendly Giant, the show treated children with respect and assumed that they would like to have fun as well as learn. The show also had puppets Casey and Finnegan who along with their puppeteer Judith Lawrence came from the Butternut Square show. Following the retirement of Casey and Finnegan, Karen Valleau and Trish Leeper were added to the cast. In common with Friendly was the very talented puppeteer Nina Keogh also joined Mr. Dressup as Truffles having been the music room puppets on Friendly. Nina has performed on many Canadian productions and has been a guest puppeteer on Sesame Street on PBS.

Size Small was a 1982 creation by the Lumbly family that featured Helen as Miss Helen, John Lumbly Jr. as Oliver, Lisa Lumbly-Richards as Grandma Gussie and Jeff Lumbly as Tex. It had a combination of music and story with a number of puppet characters. It evolved into Size Small Country in 1983 and Size Small Island in 1986. It was produced in Canada and was featured on some PBS stations.

In the 1980s and 1990s, the talents of Sharon Hampson, Lois Lillienstein and Bram Morrison gave us both the Elephant Show (1984-1988) and later Skinnamarink TV that featured a wide range of music and adventures. The silent elephant was played by Paula Gallivan. Entertainer Eric Nagler also was often part of the show. The show had both a light and vaudevillian quality to it. All the performers had high energy and good voices that made the music work well in the context of the show. Like Bob Homme, Sharon, Lois and Bram received The Order of Canada. The shows were variously on CBC, TV Ontario as well as Nick Jr.

Another remarkable performer who exemplified a positive connection with children is Fred Penner. From 1985 to 1997, Fred Penner's Place was on CBC and for part of the time Nickelodeon as well. Viewers will remember Fred with his backpack on wandering through nature with a huge smile as he took in the beauty around him. Then he would climb through his famous hollow log and into the clearing where the show would then begin. Whatever else was happening in each episode, you could be sure that you would see Fred enjoying the music he was performing. The one song most closely identified with him was The Cat Came Back. Like Bob Homme, Fred Penner was awarded the Order of Canada. Fred Penner's Place represented some continuity in quality children's programming at the CBC.

Under The Umbrella Tree was a delightful show featuring the very versatile and talented Holly Larocque who as Holly Higgins would interact with a number of puppet characters in sketches involving a story line with a theme or topic and sometimes music as well. There was always a light and humourous touch to the production reflecting not only the writing but the skills of Holly and her easy interaction with the puppet characters. The main puppets were Iggy Iguana, Gloria Gopher and Jacob Blue Jay. The show was created by master puppeteer and puppet designer Noreen Young and was produced from 1986-1993 and later co-produced with the Disney Channel until 1996. It ran in Canada from until 1997 in syndication. Iggy was performed by Bob Stutt and Stephen Braithwaite was Jacob. Noreen Young has received the Order of Canada in recognition of her talents and work along with many other awards.

The CBC in particular has made a tremendous contribution to children's television by nurturing and promoting that which was truly world-class. Individuals like Dr. Fred Rainsberry had both the education and the insight to recognize high quality programming and then gave the programs a safe place to be and to grow. Centralized programming and the high cost of production make it increasingly difficult for any network to create the kind of programs that grew out of the local television stations and contributed so much to the children of Canada and beyond.

Perhaps some of the specialty children's or nostalgia channels can bring back some of these shows to provide Canadian content, a quality alternative to what most kids watch now and a link to our Canadian roots.

31

The Golden Age of Children's Television In The United States

In the United States – the changes over the time Friendly was on-air in North America is just as startling. It was a dramatic period of history from when The Friendly Giant was created in 1954 until it finished in reruns in the mid-1990s. The United States went from President Eisenhower to Presidents Kennedy, Johnson, Nixon, Ford, Carter and Reagan (with Presidents G. H. W. Bush and Clinton if you count the re-runs). We went from the Cold War through Vietnam, Watergate to the fall of the Berlin Wall. The space race became President's Kennedy's goal to have "a man on the moon in this decade" to the "One small step for man" to the seemingly routine and sometimes tragic Space Shuttle program.

Captain Kangaroo had an enduring quality like The Friendly Giant. Featuring Bob Keeshan (also the original Clarabell The Clown on Howdy Doody) and Hugh Brannum as Mr. Green Jeans, this show also involved interaction between principal characters and puppets. The setting for the show was The Treasure House and there you would meet characters like Bunny Rabbit who lived in his hutch and was forever finding ways to con the Captain and Mr. Moose who was famous for his knock-knock jokes and buckets of descending ping-pong balls. Dancing Bear was another regular character as was the sleepy Grandfather Clock who would awaken as everyone shouted "Grandfather!" This show also featured stories and music as well as cartoons like Tom

Terrific. As The Muppets would later do, Captain Kangaroo had many celebrity guests from all parts of show business. Those of us who also grew up with The Captain remember his enchanting theme song with its bright violins as The Captain opened the little windows on the front door to peak through and then with his huge ring of jingling keys he would walk us over to where that adventure would begin. The show was aired on CBS from 1955 to 1984. Like The Friendly Giant, it also aired on public television. In the case of Captain Kangaroo, it was on PBS for six years after leaving CBS whereas The Friendly Giant began on public television in the United States before moving to Canada.

Romper Room was another early children's show that had longevity. It was originally created in the United States in 1953 with "Miss Nancy" Claster. It was unusual since it was both franchised and syndicated eventually being in six other countries. It continued until 1994 in some markets. Canadian children watched local adaptations of the show with various "Miss ____" characters. The local hostess for me was "Miss Flora." In addition to the character Mr. Do Bee who would demonstrate the positive qualities to emulate there was also a Mr. Don't Bee to remind the children how not to behave. At the end of each show, Miss Flora and her counterparts in other markets would hold up the "magic mirror" and ask if all the children had fun that day. She would then name various children that she could magically see through the mirror. "I see Jeff and Jenny. I see Brian and Susan." With a name like Grant, I watched many times and never heard my name. My mother was kind enough to contact the station to request that the mirror tune into Grant as well as the other children. The magic worked.

Mr. Rogers' Neighborhood was a fixture on PBS with new episodes being created for almost thirty years until December 2000. As mentioned earlier in this book, Fred Rogers began his Mr. Rogers character in Canada at the CBC and took the show back to his home state of Pennsylvania. In addition to being a performer, Fred Rogers was an ordained minister specifically commended to work in children's television. His opening sequence like The Friendly Giant also opened with a town scene and included him changing into his tennis shoes and sweater. He would then begin singing a song inviting each of the viewers to be his neighbor. The show featured a combination of returning characters, special guests and puppets. He loved to promote music, art, drama and stories. He reassured his viewers that they were great just as they were – and would often extend a hug to each one.

These programs and The Friendly Giant were in contrast to the other tradition of American television that featured more slapstick humor like Kukla Fran and Ollie or circus-like action like Howdy Doody and Bozo The Clown. Within PBS, the advent of Sesame Street would change the landscape of children's programming with very overt attempts to teach children, as well as moving the pace to the ever changing very short segments that we now see as normal programming in kids' television.

PBS has continued to play a vital role in creating quality programming across the age spectrum. Children's programming has continued to be an important strength and niche for the network. With the devolution seen in so much of children's programming today, the work of networks like PBS is more important than ever.

The Friendly Giant was part of the golden age of television lost to the frenetic paced shows of today. Is it just nostalgia or that lack of thoughtful alternatives in children's programming that make us wish we could still see programs like The Friendly Giant with our children and grandchildren today? Would it not be great to have children across America be given the choice to once again – "Look up – way up!" as part of their childhood days?

Growing up in Detroit in the early 1960s, I was lucky enough to see Friendly and his puppet pals twice a day, on CKLW-TV9 in Windsor and on Channel 56, Detroit's NET channel. While I was a big Friendly fan as a kid, I became an even bigger fan as an adult. Bob Homme's soothing voice and wonderful music make this show a classic.

Ed Golick, www.detroitkidshow.com

32

Friendly & The Canadian Myth

Generations of English Canadians have debated and sometimes despaired at our lack of a national identity. We're not really Americans. We're no longer British. We're not French. We do love maple syrup and hockey. Culturally, some excellent actors, comedians, musicians, authors, reporters, news anchors and business writers have come from Canada. We've had our share of inventors, academics, business successes and diplomats. Sadly, we often recognize or acknowledge our best only when they've left Canada and are recognized as successful by the U.S. or others. Then we are ready to embrace them and profess that we knew that they would be great all along.

But mostly we've been defined as a country of "not." We are the alpha-negative nation. Even our auto-answer to the passing question, "How are you?" is an uncommitted "Not bad." If people from Missouri need to see it to believe it (the "show-me" state), Canadians need to see it and have it guaranteed. If one Canadian does rise too high or too fast we need only think of the lobster joke. A lobster fisherman comes into the fish store to deliver his lobsters. One pail is covered and the other is not. The fish store owner asks why one pail is uncovered, "Won't the lobsters get out?" The fisherman assures the store owner that all is well. "These are Canadian lobsters – if one of them tries to climb above the rest, the others will pull him back down."

Noah Richler in his interesting book, "This Is My Country – What's Yours?" explores a range of Canadian novelists to try to understand what the Canadian myth or story tells us about how we see ourselves and our country. He reviews our battle with nature, our feeling that power is always elsewhere and that maybe Canada is nowhere – and that might be a very good thing.

In an age of Tom Friedman's work, "The World Is Flat" there is a sense of unease for Canadians who watch competition move from Japan to China and India. The flat earth has meant competition is no longer for just automobiles but for goods and services that can now be ordered and tracked instantly with the internet. Many Canadians wonder how Canada will compete in this new global economy. All of these uncertainties feed into our continuing lack of cohesive identity that we associate with other countries like the United States.

What are the touchstones we value? Dig a little deeper and you'll see some traits that Canadians believe or wish (as in our myth in the best sense) were true of us as a people. For Canadians who grew up in English Canada over the past couple of generations, most of the characteristics we like to rhyme off as our "national personality" are very close to the world of The Friendly Giant.

Our collective self-image seems to include seeing ourselves as tolerant people who are willing to accept the many differences in culture, ethnicity and histories. We want to learn about and understand others whether they live on the farm beside us, the town down the road or come from the other side of the world.

In a noisy world, we are quiet people, the last group who wish to grab the spotlight or be loud in any setting other than a hockey game. We are the hobbits of Tolkien's world who would enjoy food, drink and a great shaboo gathering over the power plays and machinations of countries who have national histories of conquest or empire. Canada is all about the middle way – as a middle power should.

As thoughtful people, we value education, an appreciation of music and prefer the diplomatic and personal approach. We would like to be seen as a peaceful and relational people. We're the peacekeepers from the United Nations in the blue berets.

Perhaps the couple of generations influenced by Friendly in English Canada during those formative years are products in part of those Friendly values. Maybe, just maybe, it is that we are in synch with the Homme philosophy. Either way, the magic of The Friendly Giant is part of, not just our national identity, but our national character too.

CPSIA information can be obtained at www.ICGtesting.com
Printed in the USA
LVOW05s1650180713

343558LV00007B/739/P

9 780978 027506